Screw it!

By the same author:

How to Build a Robot (with your dad)

Screw it!

Traditional Male Skills That Everyone Should Know

AUBREY SMITH

Skyhorse Publishing

First published in Great Britain in 2013 by
Michael O'Mara Books Limited
9 Lion Yard
Tremadoc Road
London SW4 7NQ

First Skyhorse Publishing edition 2018

10 9 8 7 6 5 4 3 2 1

Library of Congress Cataloging-in-Publication Data is available on file.

Jacket design by Greg Stevenson
Illustrations by Aubrey Smith
Designed and typeset by Design 23

Print ISBN: 978-1-5107-3398-5
E-Book ISBN: 978-1-5107-3404-3

Printed in the United States of America

Contents

Acknowledgements

I am most grateful to Robert and Evelyn Smith, Anna and Peter Carroll, and Mr Stubbs for their assistance, and to Mathew Clayton, Katie Duce, and all at Michael O'Mara. Special and somewhat belated thanks to Aileen Nuttall and Isobel Webster for their encouragement in finding a path. And to my Mum, who is amazing.

INTRODUCTION

For all but a sexist few, the notion that a woman's place is in the home seems a little quaint. The days of a traditional divide between the sexes, when man held the title of breadwinner proudly aloft while his wife sat waiting pretty at home for his daily return are, thankfully, a distant memory. The Second World War had a lot to do with a turnabout in attitudes, when a shortage of menfolk forced many women into roles that had traditionally been the preserve of men; a raft of new skills were learned and, more crucially, a new "can do" attitude was acquired.

And now, of course, Modern Woman is free to lead her life however she may choose. Whether it's flying in the face of danger to report from a war-torn region, locking horns with heads of state as a member of parliament, or plunging her freshly manicured (only joking) hands into a pail full of water to clean windows, barely an eyebrow is raised. Everywhere one looks, she can be seen driving cars, running businesses, and even living in her own apartment, quite without the aid of a man.

And yet, despite this happy trend, what happens when said car has a flat tire or the apartment needs redecoration? DIY, it seems, is the one area where women, generally speaking, still lag behind men. But that need be the case no longer: this volume is here to redress that balance, assisting the women of today in carrying out some of these simple tasks and repairs without the need for a tradesman and, in so doing, to further the liberties so hard won by her predecessors.

So, while women of the Edwardian era were forced to chain themselves to railings to get their voices heard, I hope the only contact their modern-day counterparts will have with such balustrades is to give them a good going-over with a wire brush, followed by an even coat of the most appropriate and durable gloss enamel.

TOOL TIME

Before undertaking any DIY you must ensure you have the right tools for the job. Don't be tempted to buy floral-handled screwdrivers and so forth as they are not intended for heavy use. Make sure you use the right tools—substituting with the wrong tool will not only give unsatisfactory results, it will also render the tool useless for its intended purpose. The most common victim of this is the humble flat-headed screwdriver—often pressed into service in place of a chisel, the poor screwdriver will not only show reluctance for the job at hand, but will also be so damaged it will no longer be able to engage with a screw.

When buying tools it isn't always necessary to buy the most expensive, but the cheapest should generally be avoided. Very cheap tools are a false economy, rarely of a sufficient quality to survive more than a few uses. It's far wiser to invest in a well-made tool from a trusted manufacturer; with proper care and correct use it should never need to be replaced and will therefore save you money in the long run. In cases where a more expensive power tool such as a circular saw is needed ask yourself how often it's likely to be of use—it may be more prudent to hire than to buy.

Kitting Yourself Out

In my mind, no home should be without the following tools and equipment.

A level

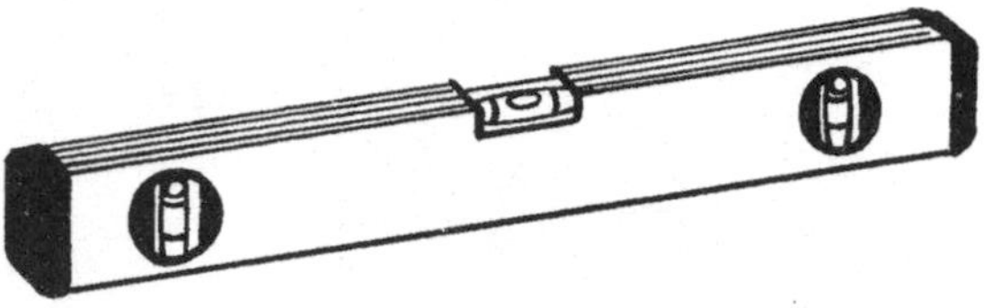

An invaluable instrument used to determine whether a surface is truly horizontal (level) or vertical (plumb), the level is a long, slim, box-like construction (traditionally wooden, now usually aluminum) into which are fitted three small glass vials—one at the center to check the horizontal level and two at either end to check the vertical. The vials are partially filled with alcohol, leaving space for a bubble to form. Because the tubes are slightly curved, the bubble comes to rest at the center when level. Although levels come in various sizes, a length of 24 inches is about average and will suit most jobs.

A power drill

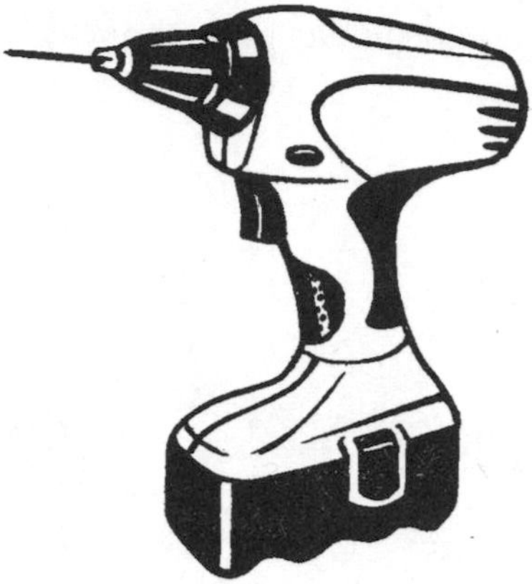

The choices are endless when it comes to electric drills, but I would recommend opting for something cordless. Because they are powered by an external battery pack, cordless drills are especially useful when it comes to working outside, up a ladder or in rooms where there are no power points. And many come with a spare battery pack, which can be charging while you drill.

Where you wish to drill into masonry, such as brick or concrete, you will need a drill with a hammer-action setting. In instances such as these a combination drill is useful as it will allow you to drill, hammer drill, and drive in screws.

You'll require different drill bits for different materials. But if all this sounds a little intimidating, worry not—

most drills bought new will come with a selection of bits, and there are only two bits that need concern you:

1. A twist bit is the most common type and will drill into wood, plastic, or plaster.
2. A masonry TCT (tungsten carbide tip) bit should be used for drilling into solid walls.

If in doubt, ask the tool store for advice.

Safety First

1. Avoid wearing loose clothing and tie any long hair back.
2. Try not to touch the drill bit after use—it will be hot.
3. Beware of electrical wires, especially if drilling into the floor or the wall.
4. Remember to replace any broken or defunct drill bits.

A screwdriver

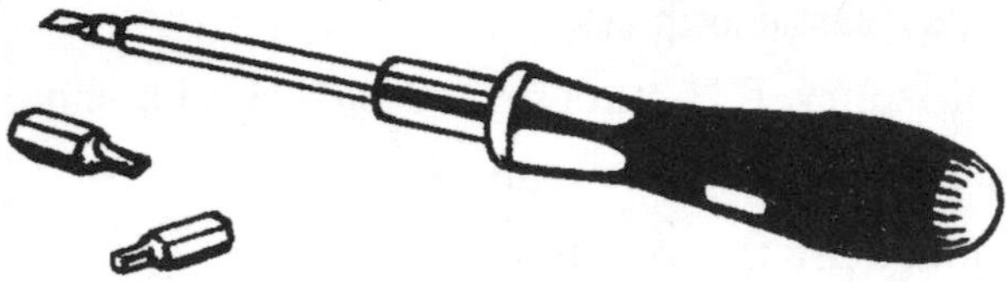

You would be forgiven for thinking there are only two types of screwdriver—the flat-bladed type and the cross-shaped Phillips type. However, there are in fact a number of subtle variations in head design, and it's important to use the correct one. Using an incorrect head risks damaging the screw on the way in, making it difficult to later unscrew.

A small but wise investment is a Stanley ratchet screwdriver, which comes with ten detachable screw bits, all of which store neatly in the handle. By always having the correctly patterned head, you can avoid any unnecessary grinding, and gears within the ratchet mechanism allow you to drive in a screw without removing the driver from the screw between each turn.

Saws

While the idea of owning a collection of saws might seem a little intimidating to the uninitiated, it's worthwhile investing in five basic types of handsaws:

1. A cross-cut saw is good for cutting across the grain of wood.

2. A tenon saw is a type of backsaw. Its rigid edge opposite the cutting edge makes it stable and affords you greater control. Used with a miter box, a tenon saw allows you to make a neat cut at a precise angle.

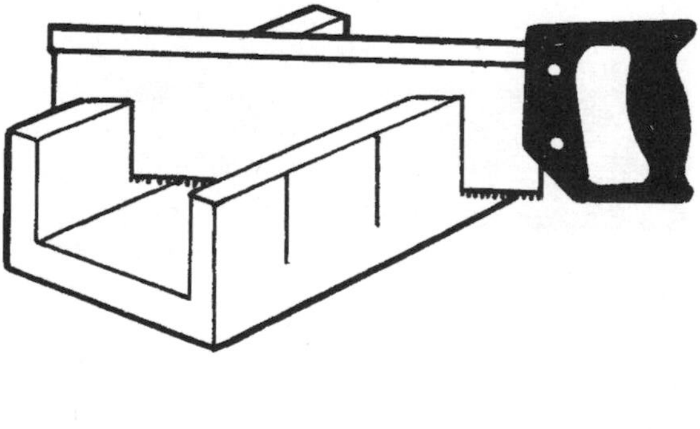

3. A hacksaw is fine-toothed with a disposable blade set within a frame. It's useful for cutting metal and plastics such as pipes.

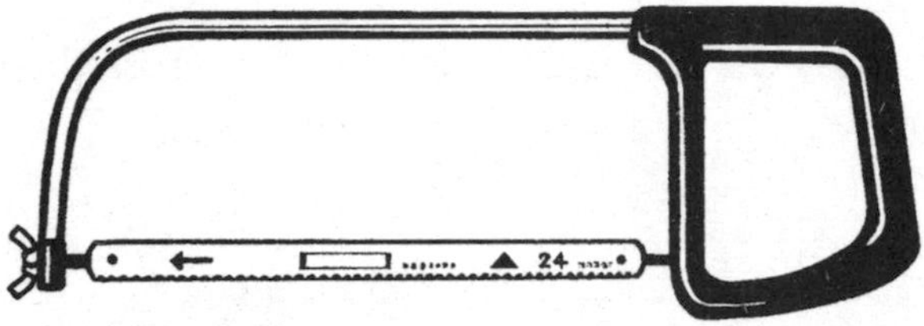

4. A ripsaw is a coarse saw, good for making cuts along the grain of wood.

5. A bow saw has a light frame and a narrow blade. It's most often used for removing tree branches (see p.98) and cutting them into firewood.

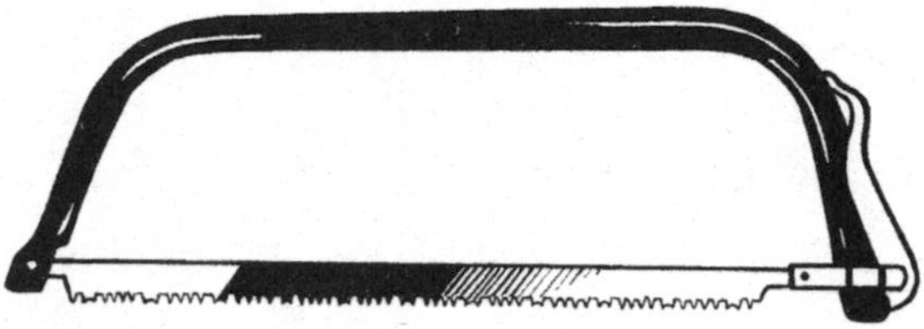

The Art of Sawing

There is something of a knack to making a straight cut in timber. With a good-quality handsaw and a bit of practice on some off-cuts you should soon become confident. Most cuts you'll wish to make will be across the wood grain and will therefore require a saw with a cross-cut blade. Where cuts are to be made along the grain, a ripsaw blade should be used.

There are obvious safety considerations when sawing: reclaimed timber should be carefully checked for old screws and nails, and the task should always be performed on a workbench or similarly stable surface. A good cut will start with slow, even strokes.

When the cut gets going, pressure should be applied on the downstroke only and the full length of the blade should be employed. Avoid the blade getting too close to your body at all times—this may seem terribly obvious, but if you were to saw through a plank of wood and into your leg you wouldn't be the first.

A tape measure

For such a compact device, a retractable tape measure allows you to measure considerable lengths. Indeed, the spring mechanism that retracts the tape into its case never ceases to satisfy. It's worth buying a good, sturdy measure as you'll probably end up using this tool more than any other.

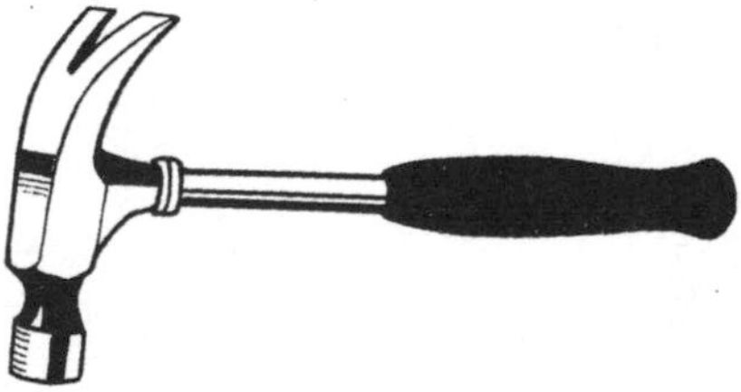

Claw hammer

A claw hammer has a dual purpose. The obvious one is to drive nails into walls or wood. Its tapered claws can be used to grip and then prise the nail out again. It is advised that safety glasses be used when hammering to protect your eyes from potential splinters. A more obvious safety consideration is that of your thumb.

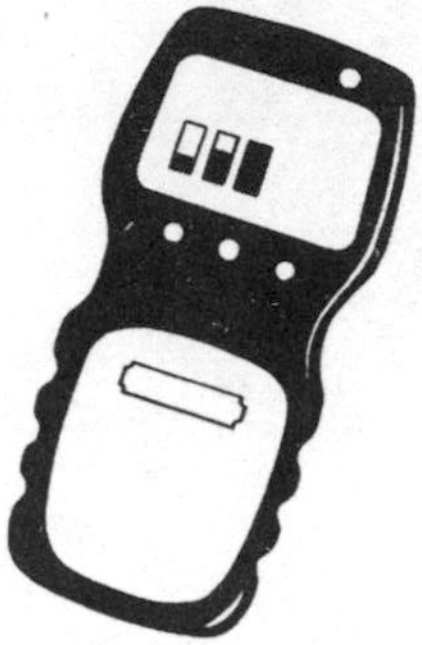

A wire, pipe, and stud detector

This handheld device is essentially a mini metal detector. When drilling into an interior (or "stud") wall it's good to know where *not* to drill. Please see page 33 for more.

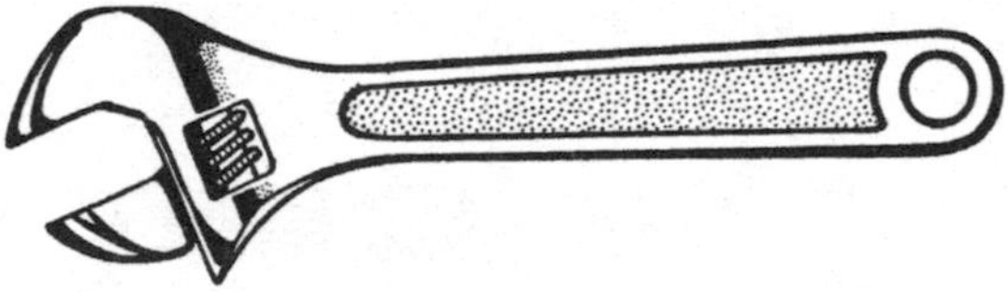

An adjustable wrench

An adjustable wrench has a "jaw" which adjusts to fit tightly around the nut or bolt you wish to tighten or loosen. Its chief use in the home is for plumbing jobs.

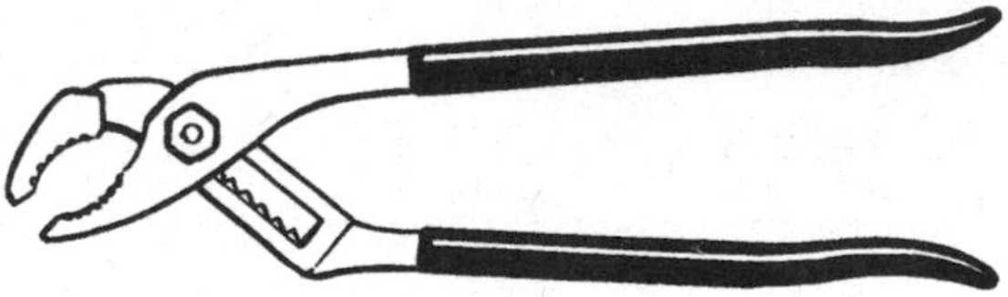

Adjustable pliers

Also known as "tongue and groove pliers," adjustable pliers can be used in much the same way as an adjustable wrench, but are also very useful when you wish to clamp or grip awkwardly shaped objects.

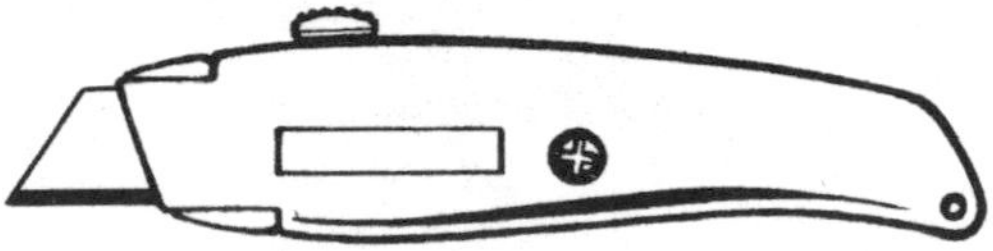

A Stanley knife

The short, replaceable blade of a Stanley knife is razor sharp, very durable, and cheap to replace. You can also get double-ended blades, which means that when you've blunted one end (which takes some doing) you can simply reverse the blade to give a new keen edge. Good news for fans of health and safety: the best thing about a Stanley knife is the blade is retractable when not in use.

A multi-tool

The best-known multi-tools are the Leatherman and the Swiss army knife, but there are a broad range of these products incorporating a wide variety of useful tools, from knives and scissors to pliers and wire strippers. Helpfully, each one folds away into a pocket-sized unit. This is a tool so endlessly useful I rarely keep mine in the toolbox—I prefer to have it on me wherever I go.

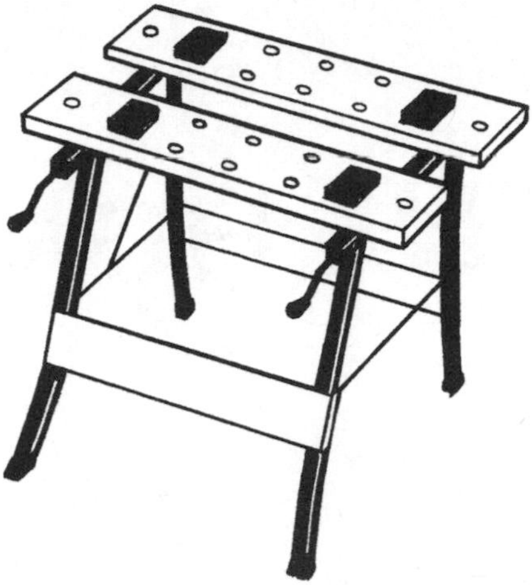

A workbench

While every handyperson deserves a workshop or shed in which to hide away, such a cumbersome structure might not be feasible when you're starting out. Where space is at a premium, a compact folding bench will provide both a work area and a good stable surface on which to tinker. A basic bench can be bought quite cheaply and is particularly useful for clamping timber in place for sawing.

Legend has it that the inventor of the folding workbench was inspired to devise it after he sawed through a chair he was using for just this purpose.

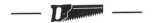

THE HOME

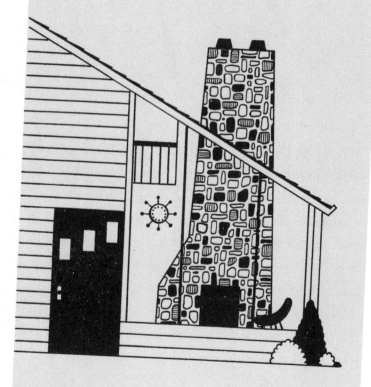

Home should be a sanctuary from the chaos of the modern world, a nest in which to unwind. But it's difficult to relax from the stresses of a hard working day if you're relying on someone else to make your house nice for you.

This chapter shows you how you can achieve a home that's both functional and attractive; a refuge in which you're as much pleased to entertain guests as you are to unwind alone. Addressing some of the more common tasks and repairs needed to make an abode function, this chapter gives you the tools you need to make your house a home.

Putting up a Board and Bracket Shelf

These days possessions, both practical and ornamental, seem almost to acquire themselves. If left unattended, books, shoes, DVDs, and electrical goods will breed and, without proper storage, begin to organize themselves into precarious towers that take up every available surface. In an effort to stop your book collection from resembling a game of giant Jenga, it's time to learn how to put up a sturdy and level shelf—which, in my opinion, is one of the simplest yet most satisfying of tasks.

This straightforward, classic shelf is an easy project to tackle. All it consists of is a length of wooden board resting on two L-shaped metal brackets secured to the wall by screws.

Tools and materials

a wire, pipe, and stud detector
a level
a power drill
a screwdriver
2-inch multipurpose wood screws
a shelf
brackets

1. Before you begin, check if there are any electrical cables, gas, and water pipes or wooden studwork behind your wall. While it's safe to assume that most shelves will be attached to an interior, or "stud" wall—

which, generally speaking, are hollow and made from sheets of drywall fixed to vertical wooden supports (the "studs")—we wish to avoid at all costs drilling into electrical cables or water pipes, so it's wise to check. As a general rule, cables run directly up or down from light switches or wall lights. However, nothing should be taken for granted, especially in an older house. I would recommend purchasing a wire, pipe, and stud detector, a relatively inexpensive gadget, which, when placed on a wall, will detect any obstacles lurking behind it.

2. Determine roughly where you'd like your shelf to go and then locate the wooden studs within the wall. Mark their location lightly in pencil. Now you know where you may safely fix your brackets.

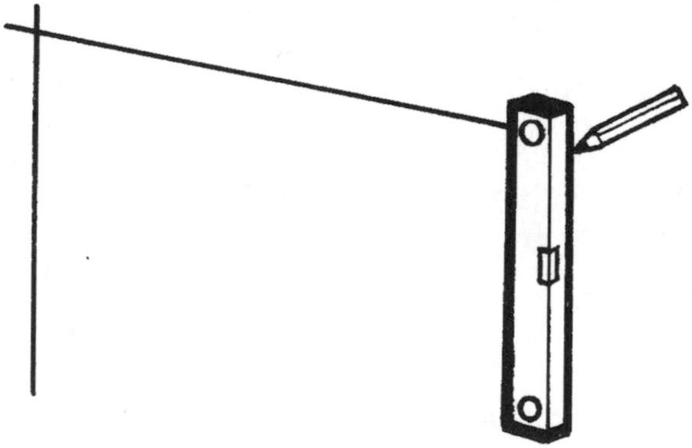

Select the height at which the shelf is to go and use your level to draw a horizontal line. With this line as your guide, use your level to draw a vertical line downwards. This will be where your brackets go. Do bear in mind that the brackets should be positioned a little way in from the ends of the shelf in order to better distribute the weight.

3. Hold one bracket in position, matching the top of it with your horizontal line, and carefully trace with a pencil where the holes for the screws are. Use the tip of one screw to make a little notch in the center of each pencil mark—this will help when you come to drill the holes. Repeat for the second bracket. Please note that if you want to fit a longer shelf, more than two brackets might be needed to help ease the strain on the outer two and to prevent your shelf from sagging in the middle.

4. Now for the fun bit! Attach a wood drill bit slightly narrower than your screws and drill a hole in the center of each pencil mark. You'll need to go through the drywall and into the stud to about the depth your screws will reach (2 inches should be about right).

5. You can now position the bracket and screw it in using your drill, otherwise an ordinary screwdriver is fine. Repeat the process for the second bracket.

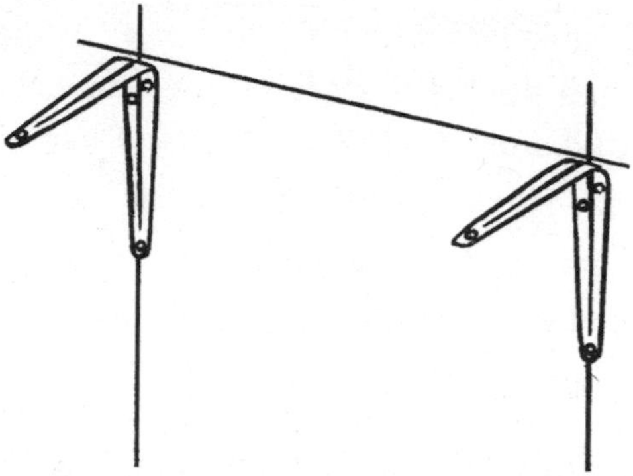

6. Now it's time to put the shelf in place. Once you're happy that the shelf is central (making sure there's an equal amount of wood either side of the brackets) screw the top of the brackets to the underside of the shelf. Make sure the screws aren't too long—you don't want to go too far through the wood and out the other side. You may also want to drill some small pilot holes in the wood first—this helps to prevent the wood from splitting along its grain when the screws go in.

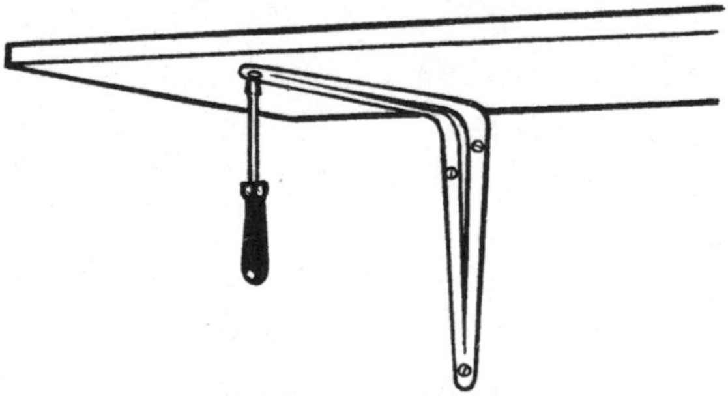

Stud Muffins

Wall studs are rarely where you'd like or even expect them to be, which can be a little annoying if you have a specific area in mind for your shelf. However, there's a simple way around this if you're not anticipating your shelf taking a great deal of weight. In this instance you can screw straight into the hollow drywall using special wall plugs that anchor themselves to the back of the board. There are a great many types available, so ask your hardware supplier for advice—and don't forget to tell them what sort of weight you expect the shelf to bear.

Shelving an Alcove

These neat little shelves look beautiful nestled inside the sorts of alcoves that often sit either side of a chimney breast. This is a slightly more advanced process than the traditional board and shelf bracket as you'll need to drill and fix into a solid exterior wall using a masonry drill bit and wall plugs. But don't worry—all will become clear …

Tools and materials

a tape measure
3 wooden battens
a tenon saw
a miter box
a power drill
a screwdriver
a level
wall plugs
a box of screws (approx. 2½ inches)
a shelf (cut to size, see step 5)

1. The first thing to be aware of is that an alcove is unlikely to be perfectly square. (Take a walk around your house with a try square and test the corners of each room—you'll find everything is a little wonky.) For this reason, we fit our supports before cutting the shelf to size. Cut a length of wooden batten equal to the width of the back wall. Then cut two battens the depth

of the alcove, making sure you subtract the depth of the long batten. With a wood drill bit, drill a hole about 1 inch from both ends of each batten, plus an extra one in the center of the longer batten.

2. Hold the long batten against the wall where you want your shelf to go and rest the level on top. Level the batten and hold it firmly in place while you draw a line in pencil along the underside. Stick a screw through one of the outer holes and make a mark on the wall where you want to drill the hole. (Alternatively you can mark the wall with a quick rev of the drill.)

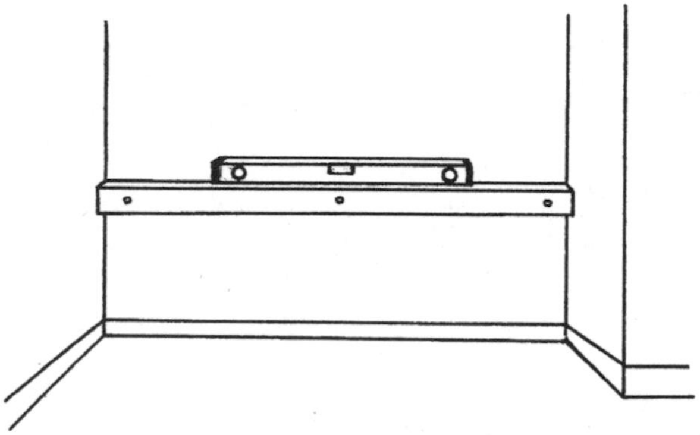

3. Put down the batten and change the wood drill bit for a masonry bit. Drill the hole you have marked and push in a wall plug (sometimes it will need a gentle tap with a hammer) until it sits flush with the wall. Please note

that when drilling into the wall your holes need not be as deep as the screws are long—you must remember to allow for the depth of the batten! Screw the batten into the hole, making sure not to screw it in all the way (you'll want the batten free to swivel up or down when you come to drill and plug the other two holes). Line the batten up with the pencil line and mark through the other two holes with a screw as before. Drill and plug these holes, then drive in all three screws fully.

4. Fix the side battens in the same manner, using the level to ensure the tops are level with the long batten.

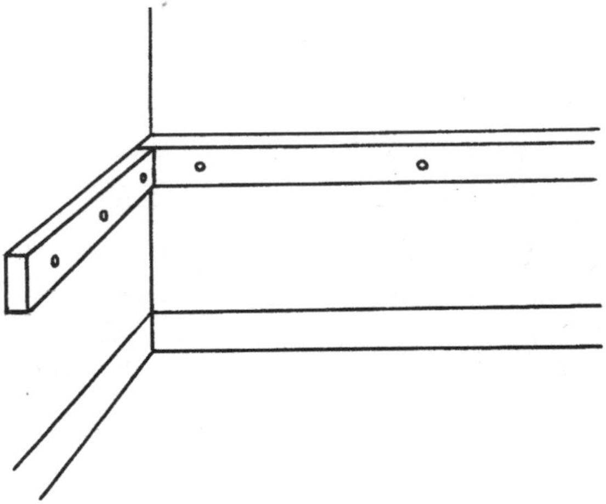

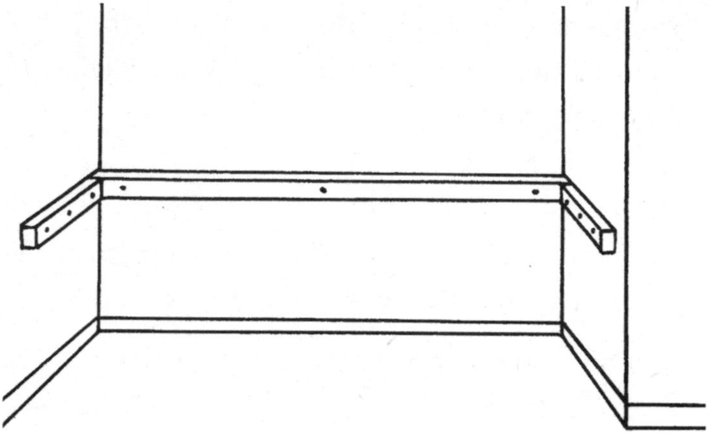

5. With the supports in place, you can now measure up for the shelf. First measure the length of the back wall, followed by the distance between the front edges of the short battens. Whichever is the shorter of the two lengths will be your shelf length. The shelf depth is that of the alcove. Once you've got these measurements, ask your timber supplier to cut the shelf to size.

6. Once the shelf has been cut, put it in place and strengthen it by screwing it on to the battens from above, taking care to avoid the horizontal screws you've already driven through.

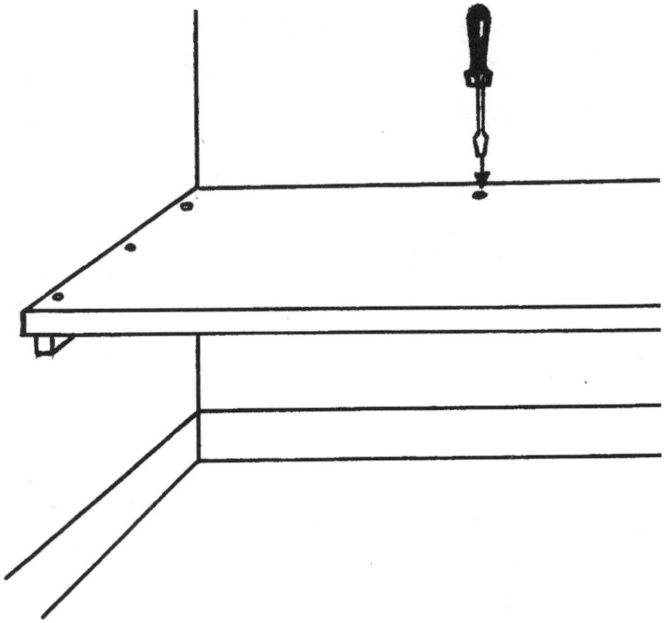

Get the Look

You may wish to cut the front edge of the side battens at an angle, as shown here (see also tenon saw on page 21). This is purely an aesthetic consideration and isn't essential.

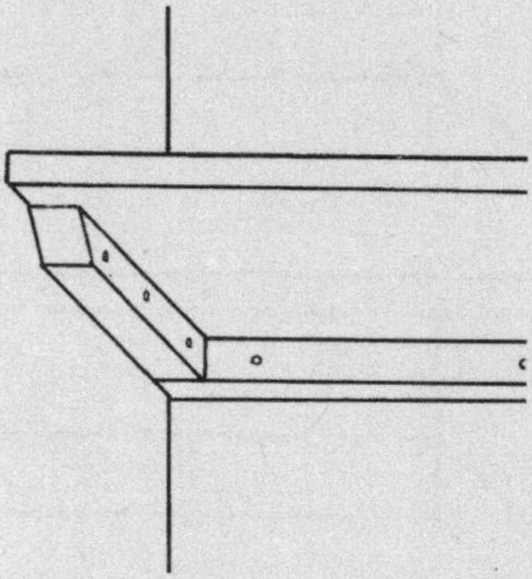

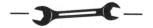

Hanging a Picture

Hanging a picture may sound like the easiest of DIY tasks; *surely it's just a matter of banging a nail into the wall?*, you may ask yourself. Well, yes, this is certainly not an uncommon approach, and in many cases may serve perfectly well. But if you want to hang heavy pictures or mirrors, and be sure that they stay put, it's worth doing the job properly.

Tools and materials

picture hook(s)
a wire, pipe, and stud detector
2-inch multipurpose wood screws
a tape measure
a power drill
a screwdriver
plugs, if applicable

1. The first thing to do is find the right picture hook (which should always be used instead of an ordinary nail—they are designed to bear greater weight and will also make less of a mess of your wall.) There are two different types of picture hook:
    - These hooks are fixed to the wall by hammering in a pin. This type is suitable for interior stud walls. It will hold a light picture to drywall, but if the picture is heavy you should use a wire, pipe, and

A Heavy Load

If you're hanging a very large picture you may wish to use two hooks instead of one. Use a level to make sure both hooks are at the same height. Position them roughly half the width of the picture apart, to allow for some movement of the picture from side to side.

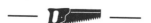

stud detector to locate a stud to fix the hook to (see figure 1).

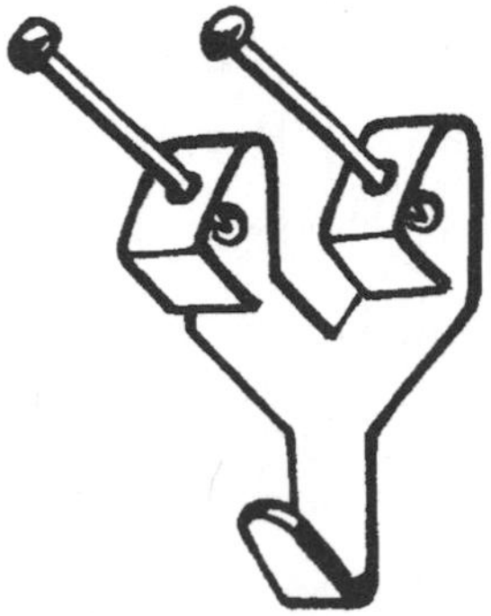

Figure 1

- These hooks need to be screwed onto the wall. They are better for fixing to exterior walls and for hanging very heavy pictures. Remember, if you're fixing to an exterior concrete or masonry wall you'll need to drill the holes using a masonry bit and insert wall plugs before screwing in the hook (see figure 2).

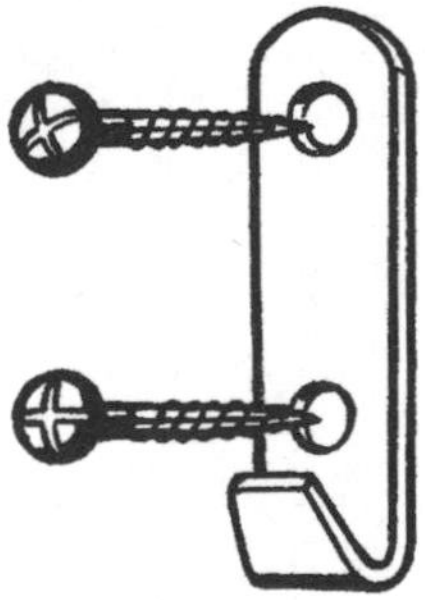

Figure 2

2. Deciding where your picture will look at its best is entirely a matter of taste, but a good rule of thumb is to hang it so the center of the picture is roughly at eye level (though perhaps not the eye level of the shortest member of the house!). Having someone else hold the picture while you stand back to view it will also help.
3. Once you've decided where it should go, make a light pencil mark on the wall just above the picture. Make sure the mark is flush with the center of the top frame. Place the picture face down and pull the wire as taut as it will be when hanging. Measure the distance from the wire to the top of the picture frame, then measure the same distance down from the mark on the wall and make another mark.

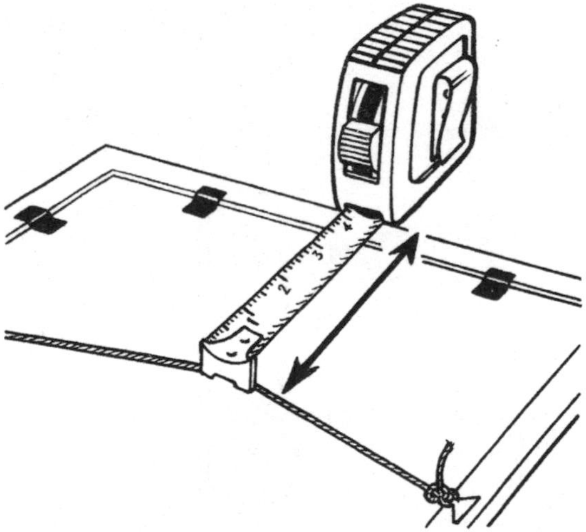

This is the point at which you'll fix your hook. Once hanging, the picture is best levelled by eye rather than with a level.

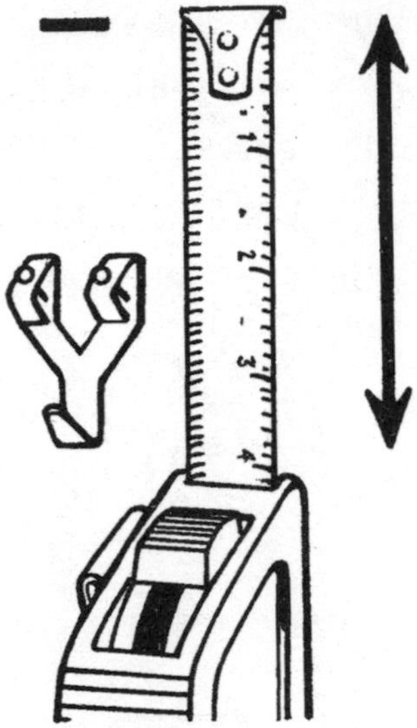

Fixing a Leaking Tap

We can all recall the slow, rhythmical "drip, drip, drip" of a leaking tap; it's enough to drive anyone mad. However, good news is at hand as it's often an easy problem to solve. A leak will more often than not be due to a worn or perished washer, which simply needs replacing. But don't let the problem slide—left unattended, a dripping tap will lose a surprising amount of water.

The variations in tap construction are too numerous to cover in detail here, so I'm going to concentrate on the most common design. Having mastered that, you should be able to apply much the same principles to other types of tap. Bear in mind you might need to take your old washer with you to a plumbing suppliers to be sure you buy the correct replacement, so it's a good idea to start this job at a time when the tap is not going to be in demand!

Tools and materials

a small screwdriver or multi-tool
an adjustable wrench
adjustable pliers
tape (electrical or masking)
a replacement washer
steel wool

1. The first and most important step is: TURN OFF THE WATER SUPPLY TO THE TAP, which is often controlled by another tap directly underneath the

sink. Next, put the plug in the sink—to avoid losing any small parts down the plughole—and turn on the leaking tap fully to drain out any water. I like to keep a cup nearby to store any small parts that might emerge from the tap as it keeps them all together and, more importantly, prevents them from wandering off.

2. Remove the cap from the center of the tap's handle using a small screwdriver or a multi-tool. You'll see that the handle is held on by a small screw. Loosen this screw and remove the handle.

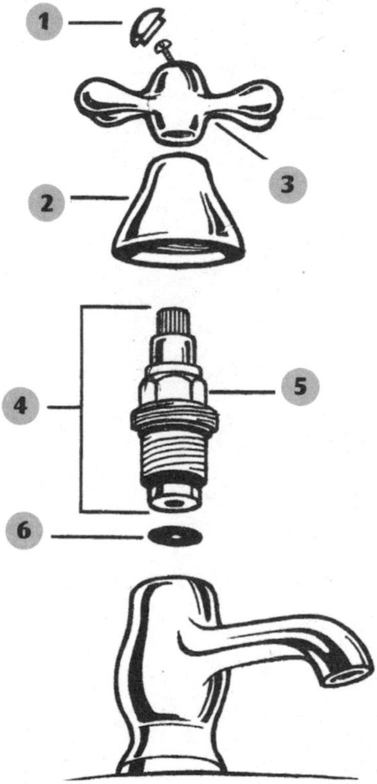

1. Cap
2. Cover
3. Handle
4. Head Unit
5. Head Nut
6. Washer

Then unscrew and remove the bell-shaped cover to reveal the valve mechanism or head unit. The top of the head unit is shaped like a hexagonal nut. Loosen this with your adjustable wrench—this bit can be tricky. You'll need to firmly clutch the spout to prevent the whole tap from turning. It may help to grasp the spout with adjustable pliers while you turn the wrench. To avoid scratching the spout, cover it with tape (electrical tape is ideal).

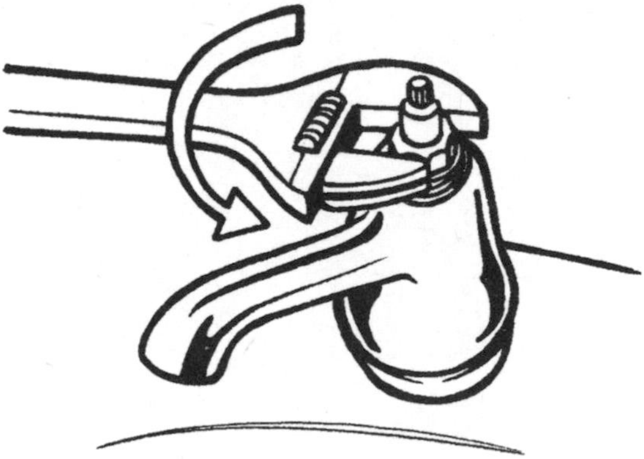

3. When the head unit is loose enough to unscrew by hand, remove it and take a look at the bottom. Here you'll find your poor old washer, which will probably be showing signs of wear and tear. In some cases the washer is held on by a small screw, in others a little nut that you can loosen with pliers.

Prise the washer out with your multi-tool and put it straight into your pocket to take to the hardware store. The replacement may be available in a single pack, or come in a pack of a few. Try to buy at least two—if your cold tap has a worn-out washer, chances are its hot neighbor won't be far behind.

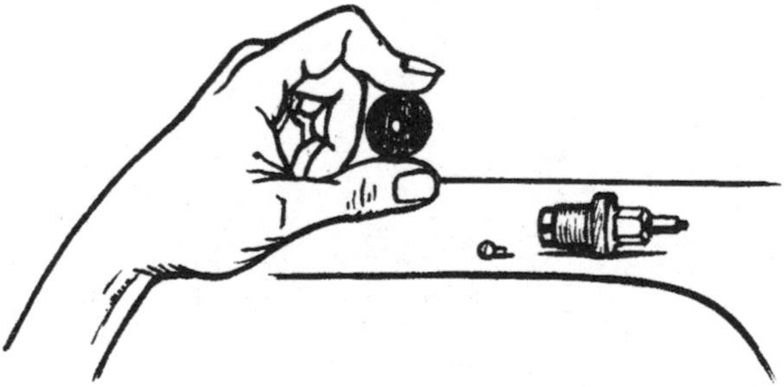

4. Before you fit your new washer and reassemble the tap, it's a good idea to give all the internal components (especially the seat where the washer sits) a good rub with some steel wool to remove any built-up grime and scale, which can add to the wear and tear.

5. With your tap reassembled, turn the water supply back on and fully open your mended tap for a minute or so. Then turn it off and you should find the drip is no more. With a final turn of the tap you can fill the kettle and take a well-deserved tea break!

Sealing a Bathtub

Along the edge of your bathtub you'll notice a rubber-like strip, which prevents water from seeping into the gap between the bath and the wall. (You'll find the same around the sink and shower tray.) This strip is a silicone sealant, which, in time, will degrade and start to peel away, exposing the wall to potential water damage. Even before this happens the silicone is prone to cultivating unsightly black spots of mildew. This growth is all but impossible to clean off; it's far better to remove the old sealant and start afresh. Although removing it does require a little patience and elbow grease, the finished look will be worth the effort.

Tools and materials

a flat blade and holder (see page 59)
WD-40
a bowl of mild soapy water
a rag
paint thinner
masking tape
a tube of silicone sealant
a silicone or caulking gun
a Stanley knife or multi-tool
a scrap piece of cardboard

Quality, Not Quantity

When choosing your new sealant, avoid the cheaper options. It's worth paying a little more for a quality, anti-bacterial sealant as it will keep mildew problems at bay for longer.

1. First and foremost you must tackle the most onerous task: scraping away the old sealant. A flat blade (hardware stores sell flat razor blades in a safety holder, which allows you to hold the blade at a near flat angle) works well to remove the silicone from tiles and ceramic baths but if your bathtub is plastic, a plastic scraper is a safer option to avoid damage. Before you begin, it's worthwhile spraying the old sealant with WD-40 and leaving it for 10 minutes. Once you're ready to strip the sealant, much like stripping wallpaper you'll find that in some sections it will come away in long, satisfying strips while other, smaller areas will prove more stubborn.

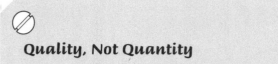

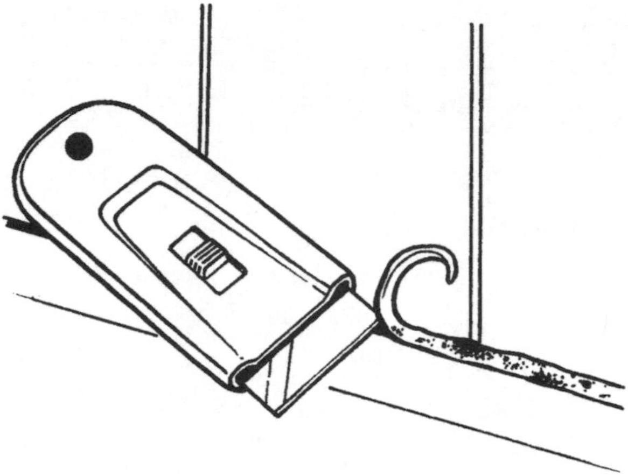

2. Once the silicone is removed, clean the area thoroughly. If you used WD-40 you must degrease the surfaces by wiping them down with a piece of rag dipped in paint thinner. When all the surfaces are clean and dry, you'll need to mark out the area where the new sealant is going to go. Run one strip of low-tack tape along the wall or tiling and one along the edge of the bath in a nice straight line, smoothing down the tape with your finger. The gap in between the two strips is where the sealant will go.

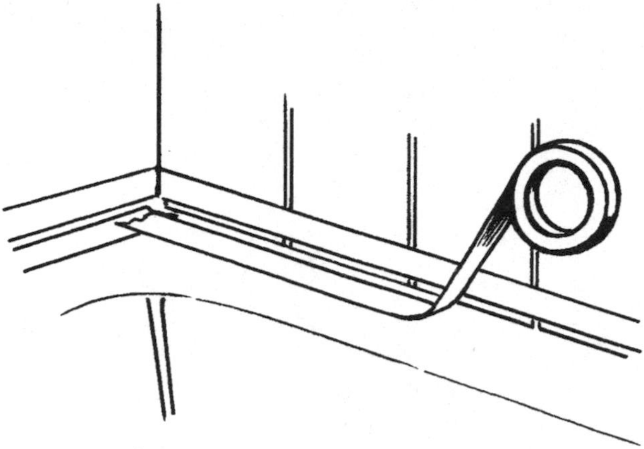

3. Sealant comes ready-to-use in a tube that fits into a silicone (or caulking) gun. Open the tube by cutting off the tip of the cap with a sharp knife (such as a Stanley knife or the sharpest blade of a multi-tool), leaving the screw thread (which screws on the nozzle) intact.

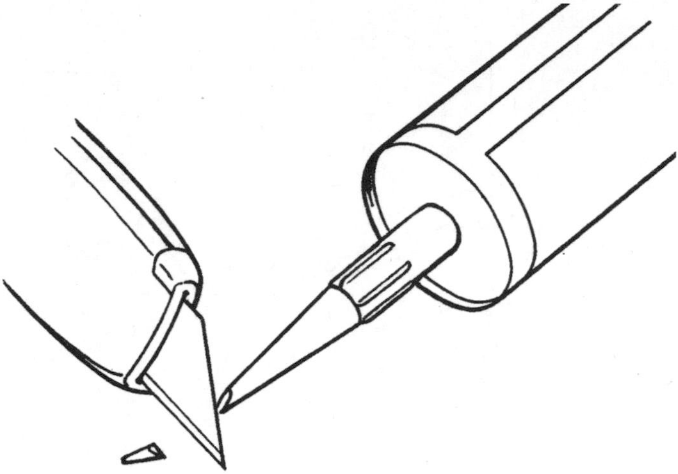

Screw on the nozzle then cut off the very tip of the nozzle at a 45° angle. How much you cut off will dictate the thickness of the bead of silicon that comes out. Load the tube into the gun, pull the trigger to squeeze out some sealant, then practise running a bead (i.e. squeezing out a continuous line along an edge) on a scrap of cardboard. The key to a good result is to move the gun along in one smooth, confident motion.

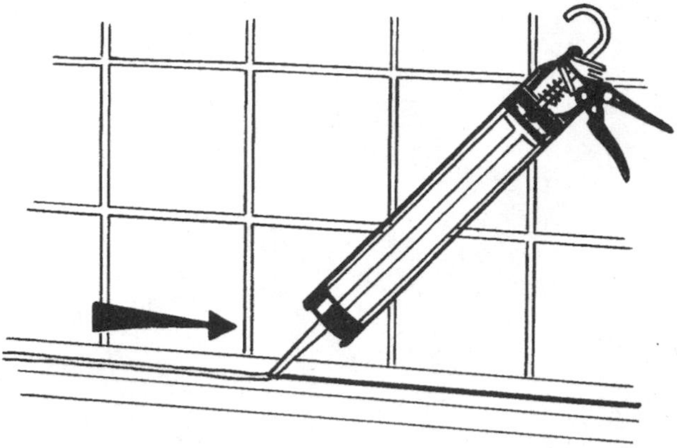

4. Once you feel you've mastered the gun, apply a nice even bead to the prepared area. Straight away, dip your finger in a little mild, soapy water and run it along the bead, smoothing the silicone to the edges of the tape. Pull off each strip of tape in one clean action and put it straight into a plastic bag to avoid any mess from the excess sealant. You should now leave the silicone to set completely before using the bath.

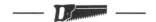

Tiling

As the old saying goes, "You can't make an omelette without breaking any eggs," which is certainly the spirit in which one should undertake a tiling job. Whatever the area you wish to tile, a certain number of tiles will most likely need to be cut to size. And, for even the most seasoned tiler, this cutting will result in breakages.

Therefore, an ideal starting point for the novice tiler is a small project, such as the kitchen backsplash, which we'll attempt here. The wall behind a stove or kitchen sink is liable to suffer the odd spattering of food and grease, as well as a great deal of water and steam. Waterproof and easily wiped clean, tiles are both a practical and attractive solution.

Tools and materials

tiles
sandpaper
a handsaw
a wooden batten
a tape measure
a level
a power drill
screws
premixed tile adhesive
a notched trowel
tile spacers
a grease pencil

a tile cutter
a pair of pliers
a sponge
premixed grout
a grouting float
silicone sealant

1. The first step is choosing your tiles. A staggering array are available in various materials and finishes: ceramic, glass, and terracotta; plain, patterned, metallic, and mirrored … and of course the prices vary greatly too. When properly applied, simple, inexpensive ceramic tiles can give perfectly effective results. But if you choose to pay a little more you may feel justified in knowing that the tiles will last a lot longer than wallpaper or paint, without fading, peeling, or blistering, so you'll save money in the long run. Once you've chosen your tiles and calculated how many will be needed to cover the space, you should buy a few extra to allow for breakages—approximately one extra tile for every ten needed. Many suppliers will refund a box of tiles if it proves surplus to requirements. And if you're buying a more expensive or unusual design, check that the supplier has more in stock and has no immediate plan to discontinue the line.

2. Before you consider tiling a wall, make sure it is a sound and reasonably flat surface, free of damp. Lightly sand the surface before you begin as this will help the tile adhesive to bond.

3. Next you need to choose which tiling method to use. There are two options:

    a. Start by tiling at one end of the wall and see what space you are left with at the other (see figure 1).

Figure 1

    b. Otherwise, and this is the option I would advise, find a central point and tile outwards so that the finished effect is symmetrical (see figure 2). Although this method will no doubt involve extra cutting, it will be easier on the eye. However, should this option result in you having to cut the outer tiles very thinly, avoid it as sliver-thin tiles are a nightmare to cut. Make a simple scale drawing on graph paper before you begin to help you avoid running into difficulties.

Figure 2

4. Start by cutting a length of batten the width of the section of wall you wish to tile. Measure and mark exactly halfway across the area and use your level to draw a vertical line at this midpoint.

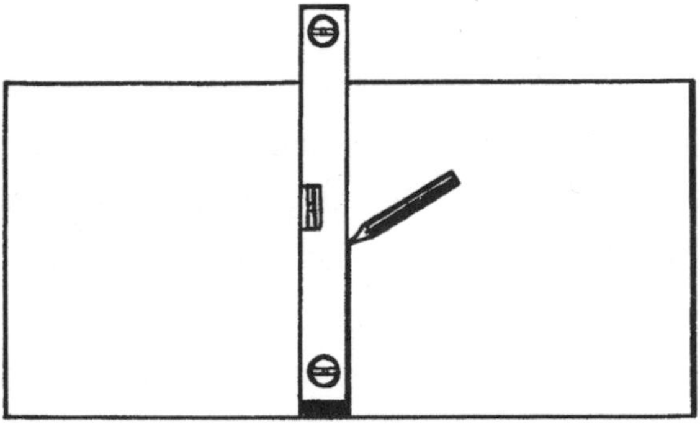

On that line, mark one tile's height from the counter top plus an extra ¼ inch (this is needed to leave a gap below the bottom tiles for the sealant). Do the same at either end of the wall, using the batten to draw a horizontal line between these three marks, remembering to check that it's level. Hold the top of the batten level with this line and screw it to the wall. The top of the batten is now acting as the bottom row of tiles, providing a level base on top of which you can start tiling.

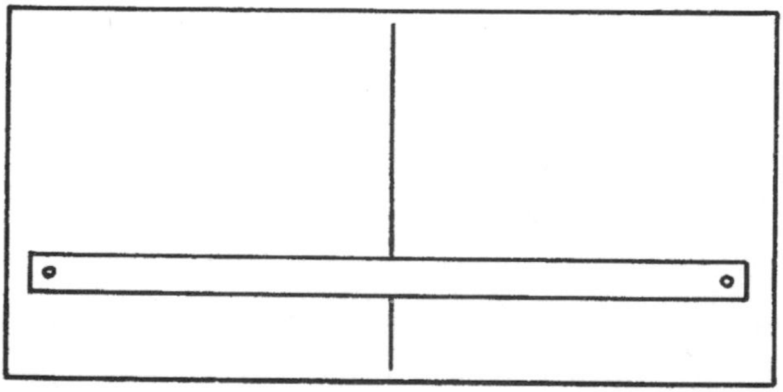

5. Now you're ready to apply some adhesive. Don't cover the whole area at once—you don't want the adhesive to start drying before you reach it, so apply enough for five or six tiles at a time.

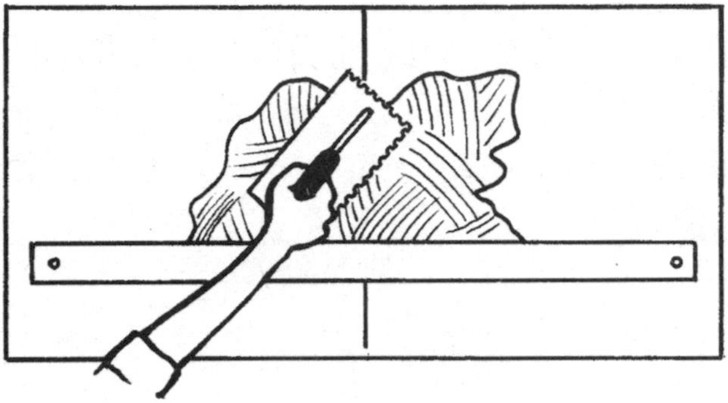

Beginning at your vertical midline apply adhesive evenly with a notched trowel. Hold the trowel at a 45° angle to make a pattern of grooves in the adhesive. Push your first tile into place next to or over the midline (depending on your pattern) and hold it just clear of the batten with spacers.

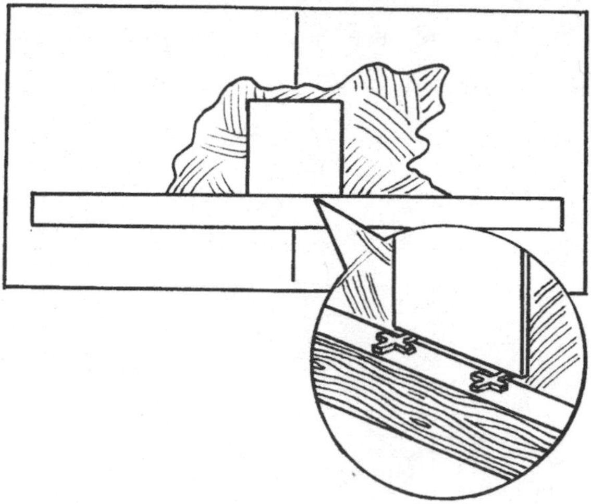

Apply the second tile in the same way with spacers between the tiles. Carry on applying tiles and spacers to cover the adhesive, then trowel on more as and when you need it.

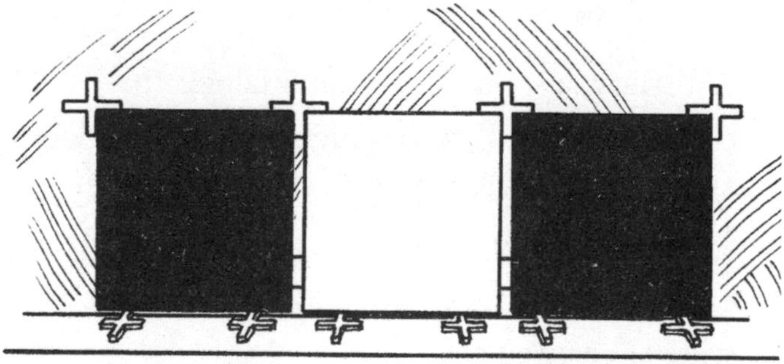

In this case, we're leaving an area of painted wall above the tiles, so when we reach the top row we'll apply the adhesive directly to the back of the tile in order to minimize the amount we have to clean off the wall.

6. To cut the outer tiles to size, hold the whole tile up to the gap and mark its face where your cut will be with a grease pencil or crayon. Place the tile in the cutter and score it with one smooth, confident action.

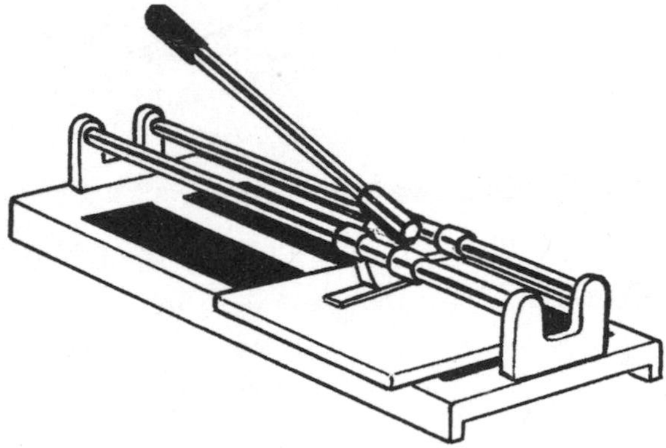

With luck, it will snap cleanly along the line. If it doesn't, you'll have joined the long and illustrious line of tile-breakers. Savor the moment then try again. Sometimes it will go well save for a few jagged teeth of excess tile, which can often be "nibbled" back to the scored line using pliers.

7. Having tiled the area above the batten, unscrew it from the wall and complete the bottom row. You may need

to use multiple spacers in the gap below the bottom of the tiles to keep them from slipping or sagging.

8. With the tiles fitted, clean off any excess adhesive with a damp sponge and leave for twenty-four hours.
9. When you've removed all the tile spacers it's time to start grouting. Apply the grout liberally to the tiled area using a rubber grouting float.

Work it into all the spaces and hold the float at a 45° angle to skim the excess grout from the tile faces. Avoid grouting below the bottom row as we will silicone seal that gap later. When all the other spaces are grouted, wipe down the face of the tiling with a damp sponge, rinsing it out regularly. As the grout dries you may notice some residue remains on the tiles. This will dry to a light dust and can be wiped off once the grout is completely set.

10. After you've left the tiles to dry for a day or two, you may apply the silicone seal to the gap between the tiling and the counter top. For this, simply follow the instructions for sealing a bathtub on page 57.

Replacing a Pane of Glass

Glazing is another job that most people would instinctively leave to a qualified tradesperson. While this is certainly advisable when dealing with a large sheet of glass, smaller panes, like those found in this four-light door, are perfectly manageable.

Safety is of course the first consideration when handling glass (broken or otherwise) and tough gloves are essential. Ideally, wear a pair that protects your wrists. And when knocking out the broken pane wear safety glasses too.

Tools and materials

an old sheet
safety gloves
safety glasses
a hammer
pliers
a small chisel or metal scraper
sandpaper
a tape measure
replacement glass
a tub of putty
a putty knife
a box of glazing points

1. Before you begin, place an old dust sheet on the ground outside the door to catch the glass. Be sure it's a sheet you're happy to throw away as it will trap tiny shards that may surprise you at a later date!

2. With gloves and goggles on, knock the larger pieces of glass out from the inside of the door with a hammer. Smaller pieces around the frame can be worked free with the pliers.

When all the glass is removed, remove the old putty from the rebate (or "rabbet"—woodworking terms for a groove) using the scraper or, if it is particularly stubborn, a chisel. Take care not to damage the timber as you strip away the putty and any old, flaking paint.

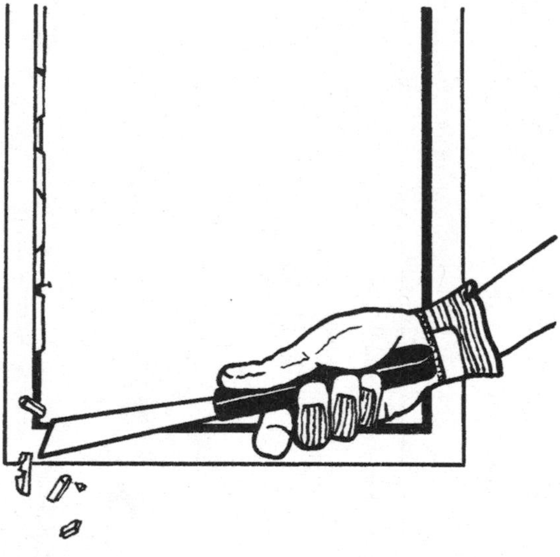

Prise out any old glazing points or nails with the pliers. If necessary, give the rebate a light sanding.

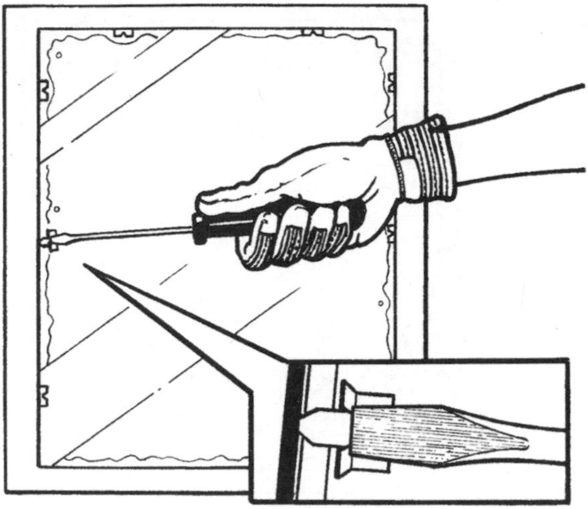

3. Now you're ready to take an accurate measurement of the frame. Measure the width and height of the rebate using your tape measure and subtract ⅛ inch to give the measurements for the new glass. (This will ensure an easy fit.) Take the thickness measurement from one of the broken pieces of old glass, making sure you handle it very carefully. You may wish to give any bare wood a quick coat of exterior wood primer at this point. It should be dry by the time you get back from buying the new glass.

4. When you have the new pane, handle it wearing gloves and with as much care as you did the broken glass as the raw edges of cut glass can make for a nasty injury. Once your frame is dry and dust-free, apply a bead of putty around the edge. Soften the putty in your hands and roll it into a thin strip, then smooth it into the rebate with your thumb. Now take hold of the pane of glass by its sides. Rest the bottom edge in the bottom of the frame and push the glass into place. Put just enough pressure on it to squeeze the putty beyond the rebate. Center the glass.

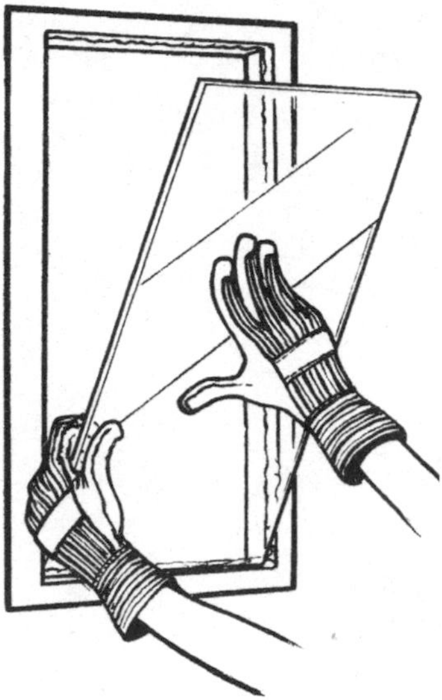

5. Now insert glazing points around the frame. These can be purchased at a good hardware store. Ask for the type which can be pushed in using the end of a screwdriver or your chisel. (Traditionally, pins were tapped in with a hammer at this point; having come this far, I wouldn't want a hammer anywhere near my new window!) Now the pane is firmly in place, apply putty all round the frame. Use the putty knife to smooth it evenly and at a consistent angle. This bevelling doesn't only look nice, it also helps the rain to drain off. Remove any excess putty on both sides of the pane. If you wish to paint over the putty, consult the tub for drying times.

THE GARDEN

Too many gardens go largely unused, which seems a terrible pity—on a fine morning coffee tastes far better drunk in the open air. If your home is blessed with an outdoor space, whether it's a tiny square yard in the center of the city or a sprawling rural wilderness, you need not be green-fingered to enjoy it. The focus of this chapter is on the practical projects you can do to turn your garden into an area you'll be more inclined to use, whether it's spending time with friends or to get away from them!

Making a Compost Bin

Whatever you choose to grow in your garden, you'll do well to feed it with home-made compost. An organic material that, when decomposed, can be used as a fertilizer to enrich your soil with the carbon and nitrogen plants need to thrive, compost acts almost like conditioner. It's a greener alternative to using chemical fertilizers and about a third of household waste can be composted. From food scraps, peelings, tea leaves, and used coffee grounds (and used coffee filters too), to grass cuttings, garden waste, paper, and eggshells, pretty much anything that's organic and will break down over time can be thrown on the heap. There are, however, some things you should avoid: bones and scraps of meat or fish are likely to attract unwanted pests to your garden; also glossy paper and paper printed with coloured inks, and weeds that have gone to seed.

Although the stores boast a range of ready-made composting bins of all shapes and sizes, you can achieve the same results by building your own very simple bin from some old wooden pallets.

Tools and materials

4 wooden pallets (of the same or similar size)
garden gloves
stiff wire or thin rope
a pitchfork

1. Gather together four pallets of a similar size, making sure you wear gardening gloves when handling them to avoid splinters. Choose a piece of level ground away from the house as the compost can start to smell rather ripe as it decomposes. Construct a box shape and fasten the pallets together at the corners using wire or thin rope. The front pallet should be fastened on one side only so that it functions as a gate when you want to access the compost.

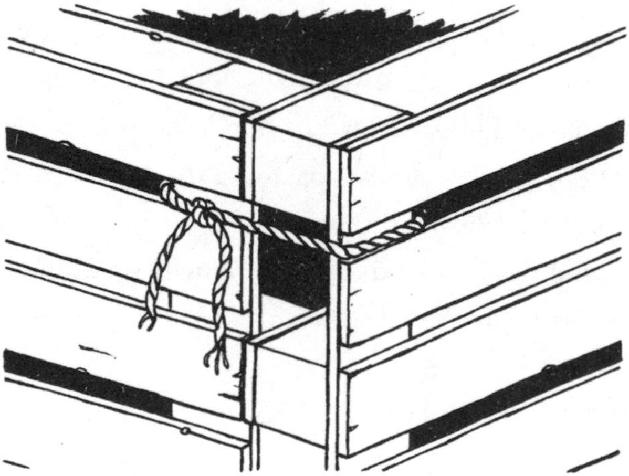

2. You don't need a base for the bin—the compost will benefit from sitting directly on the ground to allow worms to burrow up from below and introduce oxygen into the pile. Straw will help it to breathe too. Place a layer beneath the pile of compost and throw handfuls on top each time you add to it. For further aeration you should turn the whole heap over with a pitchfork every couple of weeks.

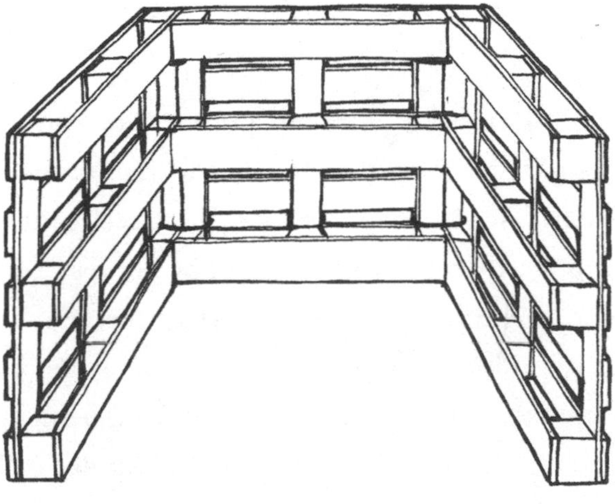

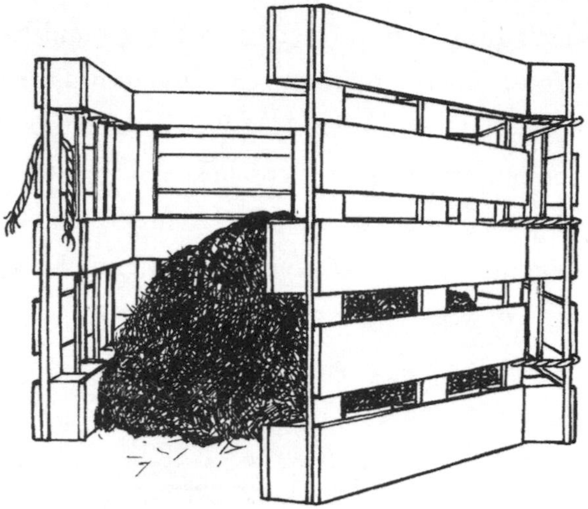

3. It's good to keep the compost moist too. I once heard a well-known British gardener and radio broadcaster sharing his own method of accelerating the decomposition process. After a few bottles of organic cider, he strolls to the end of the garden and relieves himself on the compost. One presumes his bin isn't overlooked by neighbors! This practice being a little uncouth, you might prefer to use rainwater collected in a bucket next to the bin instead.

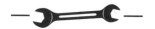

Planting a Tree

As well as adding beauty and form to a garden, trees are enormously beneficial to the environment. This is especially true in urban areas, where they play a critical role in combating pollution. If your garden is not already blessed with a tree, planting one can have positive effects immediately and for generations to come.

Careful consideration should be given to the type of tree you choose to plant and where; a tree that's going to outgrow the space you have available and whose roots, in time, are likely to damage nearby buildings is not a happy legacy. A little research should avoid any problems for you, your neighbors, and possibly your grandchildren. Fruit trees are a good choice, as much for their blossom as their produce, and they are a good option for relatively small gardens.

Please note the following are general guidelines and some species of tree will require different handling. Ask at the nursery or garden center if you're unsure.

Tools and Materials

a spade
a pitchfork
a sledgehammer
a rubber tree tie
a wooden tree stake
some mulch

1. A young tree, or sapling, is best planted in early spring or autumn to avoid exposure to extremes of temperature. When you buy your sapling it will usually be rooted in a pot or have its root ball wrapped in a net or sacking. Greater care should be taken when handling the latter to avoid damaging the roots. Mark the spot where you wish to plant and place the tree nearby.

Digging For Victory

A good-sized spade is used for digging holes in gardens. Be mindful to choose the right size for you, and not one so heavy that it makes digging even harder work. Similarly, choose a fork that is the right weight and size for you.

2. Dig a hole deep enough to accommodate the root ball while leaving the base of the trunk an inch or two above ground level so that water won't collect there. The hole should be twice the width of the roots so that they will have freshly turned and aerated soil to grow into. The outer edge of the hole should be deeper than the middle. Again, this is to allow drainage away from the root ball so it won't become waterlogged.

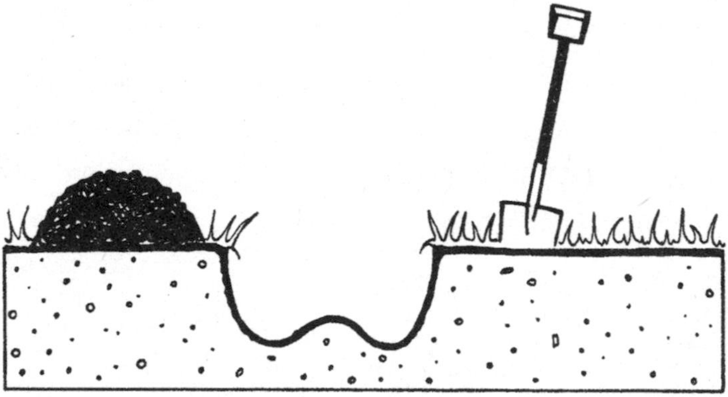

3. Now to put your stake in the ground. This is a job for two people—one of you will be holding the stake upright while the other knocks it in with the sledgehammer. This can be something of a test of trust for whichever of you is doing the holding! It may be necessary to stand on a sturdy crate to reach the top of the stake for the first few blows. Position the stake just outside the hole and drive it about a foot into the ground or until it feels rigid.

In Position

To avoid backache when in the garden, make sure the handle of your spade or fork is right for your height, and keep your back straight as you dig.

4. Having removed the tree from its pot, or the packaging from the root ball, you may now place your tree in the hole.

   Get your helper to hold it in place. Use a pitchfork to break up the soil you dug out and use it to refill the hole with the tree kept upright as you do so. Use your boots to push the soil firmly into the hole, though not so compacted that it won't allow water to drain and air to circulate. Note that we are only using soil and not adding any fertilizer, which can damage the roots of a young tree.

It's Never Too Late

If you're new to gardening, remember it's never too late to try your hand at a bit of planting. Remember, plants want to grow—that is their purpose in life. All you have to do is give them a helping hand, then stand back at let them do the rest.

Pruning a Tree

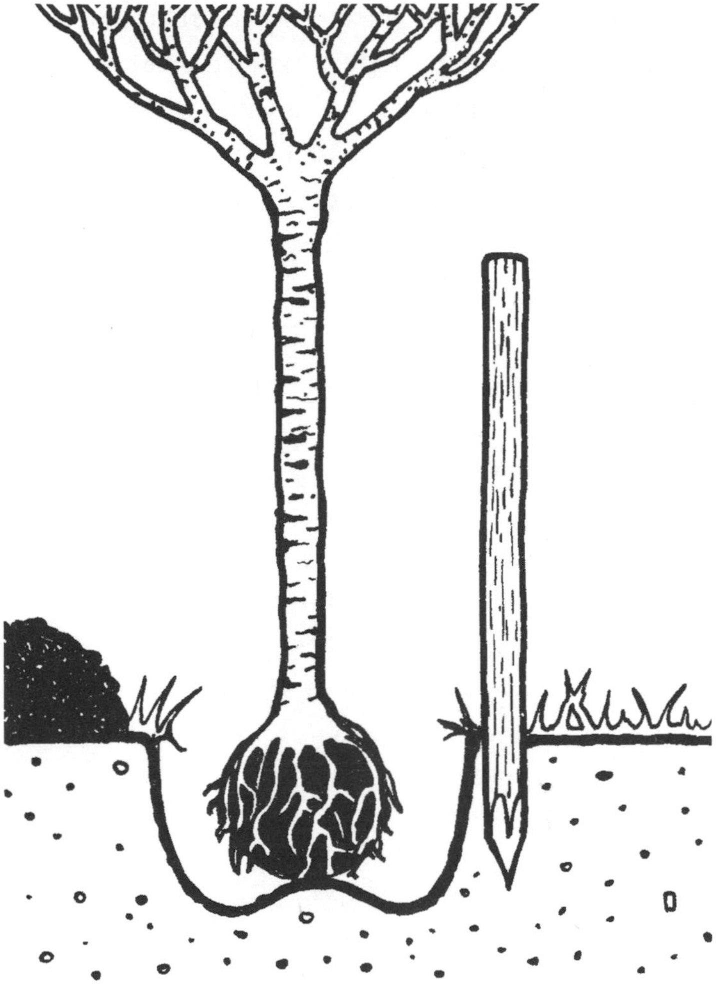

5. Strap the tree to the stake using the rubber tree ties, but don't tie them too tightly—allow a little give for the tree to move in the wind as this will help to strengthen it. Finally, surround the base of the tree with a good mulch of compost or bark shavings to help kill off any grass around the base as otherwise it would steal water and nutrients from the tree's roots.

Think Ahead

Choose the right time to plant your tree. Autumn and spring are, generally speaking, appropriate, but make sure you check the label of your tree to make sure. Remember also to choose a tree suitable to your local climate.

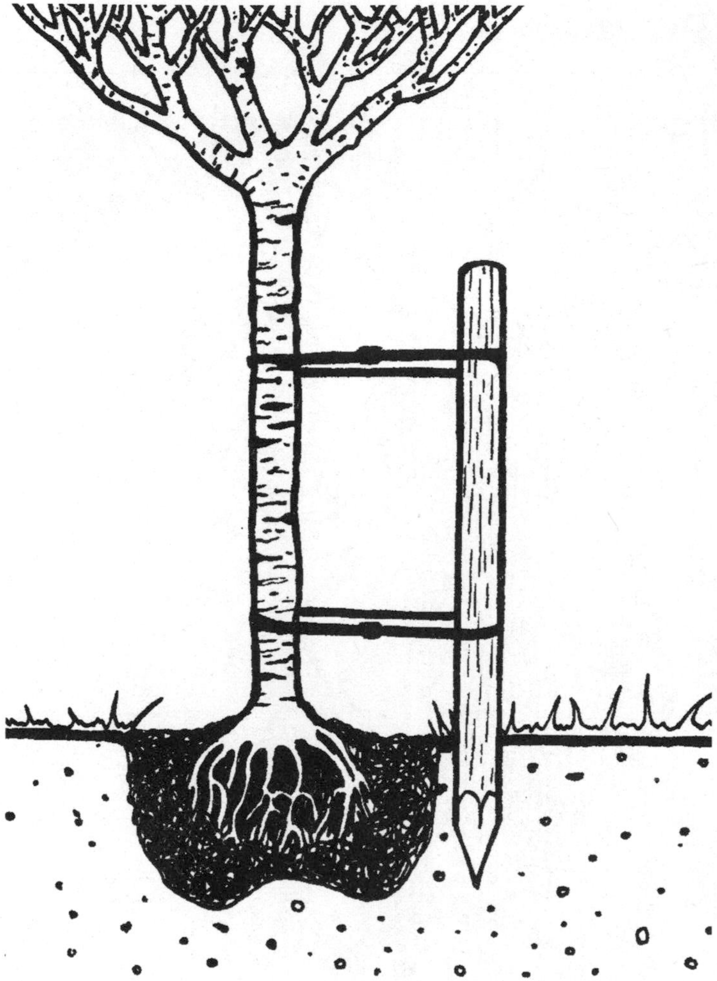

If you have well-established trees in your garden, you will have to remove branches on occasion: a limb might be dead or showing signs of disease; two branches might have grown to cross paths, rubbing against each other and leaving the tree vulnerable to diseases and pests; the tree might just be getting too big for its boots and depriving the garden of light or encroaching on boundary fences.

Whatever the reason, you should think very carefully about what you can tackle on your own. Work involving very thick branches and any work high up in the tree is best left to a professional tree surgeon as it's hard to think of many things more hazardous than using a chainsaw 40 feet from the ground with no training. In fact, I wouldn't advocate using a chainsaw at all if you haven't been taught. My advice is to attempt only lower-level work using a bow saw. And think twice about using stepladders as they're not suitable for use on soft ground. A better bet is a single ladder, which you can lean against the trunk of the tree and secure with a rope. Before you cut, think about where the branch will land and be aware that it could bounce. If the branch is very long you might consider cutting it into shorter sections. It goes without saying that children and pets should be kept out of harm's way.

Tools and materials

a bow saw (with a blade suitable for green wood)
safety glasses
protective gloves

Before you begin, it's important to make the right cuts to a branch to avoid damaging the tree. If you cut straight through the branch from above it may tear the bark as it falls, leaving the tree exposed to disease.

1. Make your first cut to the underside of the limb, approximately 6 inches from the collar, where the branch meets the trunk. This cut need only go about a third of the way through.

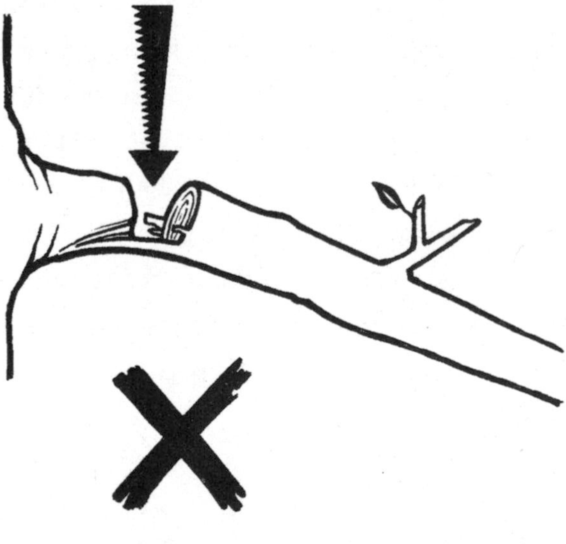

2. A few inches further along, cut right through the branch from above.
3. Make your final cut an inch or so from the collar. Angle this cut so that rainwater runs off the remaining stub.

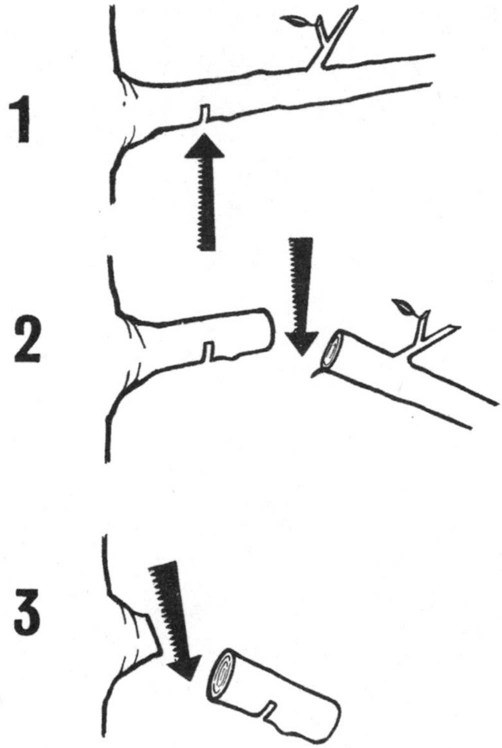

To Prune or Not to Prune?

When should you prune? In the case of most deciduous trees—those that shed their leaves annually—late autumn or winter when the tree is dormant is the best time. It'll be less prone to attack by insects, disease, and fungi and it'll be easier to see what you're doing as the tree will be leafless. Evergreens may be pruned all year round, though early spring is preferred if you want the tree to fill out with new growth quickly.

Cooking on a Charcoal Barbecue

The barbecue has a peculiar effect on the male of the species: present a man who normally refuses even to boil a potato with a rack of glowing coals and a few pounds of sausages and he'll eagerly don a chef's hat and apron in a peculiar display of territorial dominance. However, ladies, it's time to wrestle those tongs from that man and start grilling yourselves.

While cooking on the barbecue isn't as convenient as shoving something in the oven is, the flavor a charcoal barbecue grill imparts on meat and vegetables is unsurpassed. Traditionally, barbecuing works best with a low cooking temperature and a lot of smoke—cooking the food slowly helps the barbecue flavor to get into the meat.

Tools and materials

a barbecue
charcoal briquettes
newspaper
lighter fluid
long matches
barbecue tongs
a spatula
meat or vegetables for barbecuing

1. Make sure the barbecue is stood on a flat level and away from any bushes or hedgerows. You'll need a bucket full of water by the side of the barbecue.
2. The grill takes a while to heat up, so light it at least 20 minutes before you plan to start cooking. Take off the grill and pour a good layer of briquettes on to the barbecue. Scrunch up a few pieces of newspaper and tuck them inside the coals. Pour on a few more coals and arrange them in a pyramid shape.

3. Coat the coals with lighter fluid. Just enough to make them look a bit shiny is fine. Strike a long match and light the barbecue in a couple of places. Once the barbecue is lit do not pour on any more lighter fluid.

4. After approximately 20 or 30 minutes the flames should have died down and the coals should be white-hot. Using the tongs, spread the coals out along the bottom of the barbecue. A thin layer of coals can be used to cook slimmer cuts of meat; a thick layer of coals is good for searing larger pieces of meat (which you can finish cooking on the side with the thinner layer of coals).

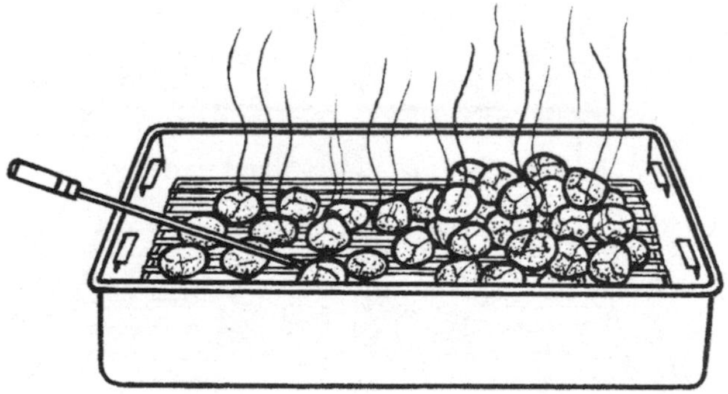

5. Using a pair of heatproof gloves, replace the grill. Now you may begin cooking your food. Keep an eye on the food and make sure you cook it for long enough—how long will depend on what you're cooking, especially if it's meat. Make sure you turn the meat regularly (using the tongs and spatula—you want to avoid piercing the

food with a fork so you don't lose any flavors) and make sure it is fully defrosted before placing it on the grill. Generally speaking, meat is ready when there are no pink bits still visible and the juices are running clear.

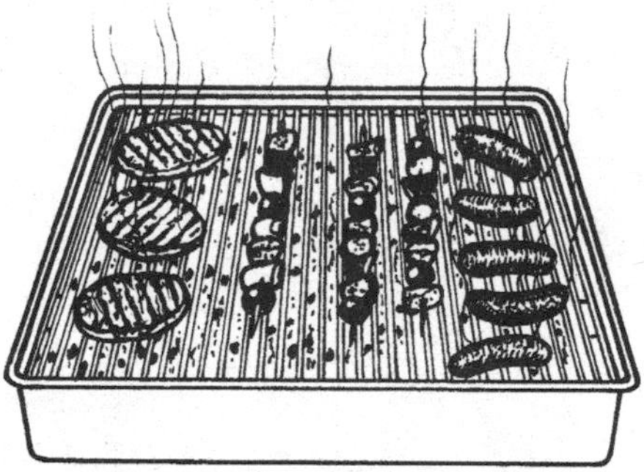

Relight My Fire

When you next come to use the barbecue make sure you clean the grill beforehand, using a wire bristle brush to remove any old bits of meat. Replace any old bits of coal and remove any ash.

CAMPING

Whether your idea of a rural retreat is an afternoon spent strolling through the woods or a week exploring a remote mountainside, there's nothing quite as restorative as a good lungful of fresh country air.

There's been a great revival in outdoor pursuits in recent years. As the fashion for cheap flights to foreign countries has receded, camping holidays have once again become popular. But if the idea of camping conjures up images of a celebrity survivalist living for months off roasted earwigs, worry not—this chapter is dedicated to far more genteel and enjoyable outdoor pursuits.

What to Take

The equipment you take on a camping trip depends entirely on the kind of experience you're looking for. Campers well versed in survival techniques, looking to rough it in a wilderness shelter, will probably pride themselves on taking little more than a sleeping bag and a good knife. At the other end of the scale is the camper with their sights set on a campsite with shower, toilet facilities, and a store. Let's assume you're somewhere in between: you're setting off for a weekend stay at a site that boasts minimal amenities. Your aim is to carry no more weight than is needed, but to be well enough equipped to stay safe and enjoy the trip.

Supplies

1. **Water:** the first thing you need to know is what water the campsite can provide. If it has fresh running water, there's little point in you taking your own, especially as it'll add significant weight to your pack. You should, however, take a small bottle of drinking water for your journey there, which can then be refilled to take on any walks you might take during your stay. A collapsible water carrier will be useful for fetching larger quantities for cooking.

2. **Food:** find out if the site or a nearby farm will sell basic provisions such as eggs and milk, and be sure you take enough cash, as a card won't cut much ice with a

farmer. Any food you do carry should be light—dried food in packages, such as instant rice or couscous dishes, are ideal. In general, avoid taking too many canned items as the weight soon adds up. That said, canned fish like sardines are fairly light, don't require a can opener and are surprisingly filling. If you want to take bread, I recommend a loaf of sliced pumpernickel—its brick-like shape makes it easy to pack and its dense texture means it's less likely to get squashed. Try to pour anything that comes in a jar into a lighter plastic container; old plastic film roll canisters are useful for small quantities like salt. Dried fruit and nuts are a good source of energy and are especially useful to keep you going on a long hike. Don't worry if what you're taking doesn't sound like the most appetizing or gourmet fare—camping will give you an appetite that makes a plate of scrambled eggs and a cup of instant coffee taste like the best breakfast you've ever eaten.

Cooking

1. **Stove:** when it comes to purchasing your gas camp stove, there are two common types from which to choose. The simplest and cheapest is a gas burner that fits to the top of a small butane/propane gas cylinder. On the plus side it's light and compact, but on the negative it's prone to toppling over. While you can make them more stable by packing earth or rocks around the cylinder, the cooking pot or kettle still feels somewhat precarious.

I prefer the second option: a flatbed double burner. It doesn't usually fit in your backpack, coming instead in a carry case. Not only does it run on a more compact gas canister, another advantage is that you can cook your eggs on one burner while you boil water for coffee on the other.

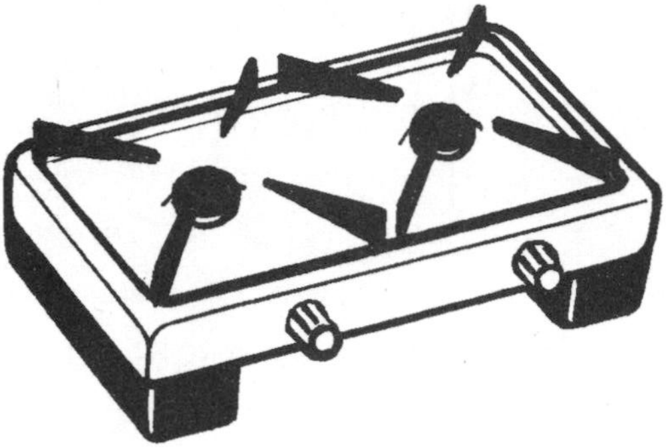

2. **Implements:** you should aim to take as few cooking implements as possible. The most compact cooking pot is a rectangular mess tin. It packs well (the handles fold inside the can) and is fine for cooking. It isn't, however, ideal for boiling water as it's quite shallow and doesn't have a lid. Instead, you should invest in a fire-safe pot with a lid, otherwise a camping kettle is just as good.

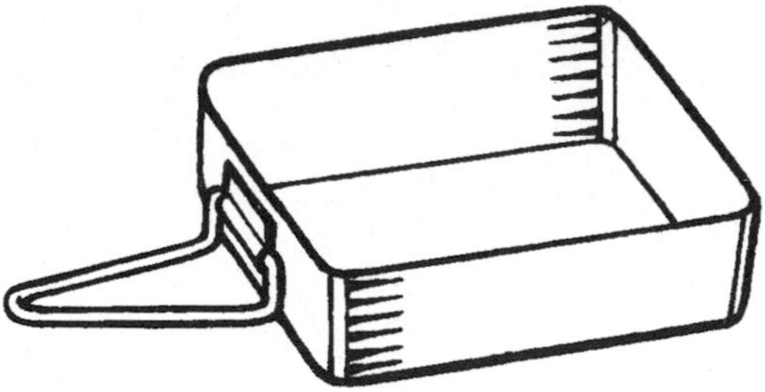

Whichever you choose, either one can be hung outside your pack if it won't fit inside. A small wooden spoon is good for stirring, and you shouldn't need more than one of each item of cutlery per person. I make do with one fork, a teaspoon, and the larger blade of my Swiss army knife. A popular option is a spork—a combination of a fork and spoon. One lightweight plate and mug per person should suffice. Finally, if you don't like eating or drinking from plastic, traditional enamelware is still widely available and is remarkably light.

Sleeping

1. **Sleeping bag:** aside from your tent, a good sleeping bag is the single most important piece of camping kit. Whether you require extra comfort is a matter of personal preference.

2. **A pillow:** if you can't sleep without a pillow, an inflatable one is the most practical option; alternatively you might, like me, be content to use your jacket.

3. **An airbed:** if you're not keen on the idea of sleeping on the ground, take an inflatable mattress. While some diehards might scoff at such luxury, if roughing it means you barely get a wink and find yourself fit for nothing the following day, then forget the endurance test.

Clothing

1. **Clothes:** what clothes you take will of course depend on the time of year. If you're only going for the weekend, the common sense approach would be to take the clothes you're standing up in plus one full change of clothing in case you get soaked. A hot, sunny day may turn into a clear, cold night, so an extra layer will be welcome when you're sat round the campfire gazing at the stars. Go for anything that's lightweight, breathable, water-resistant, and quick to dry. This rules out denim,

especially if you like to go walking, as it becomes uncomfortable in hot weather and unbearably so in the wet. I would avoid shorts as they're not much use when you happen upon a footpath overgrown with nettles.

2. **Footwear:** boots should be stout, waterproof, and breathable. New boots should be "broken in" gradually way ahead of the camping trip—if you try to break in new boots on a long walk, they'll probably break you first.
3. **A hat:** remember to take a light-colored hat for when you're out in the sunshine.

Tools and other essentials

1. **A multi-tool** is invaluable. Typically it will include a knife blade, saw blade, can opener, bottle opener, scissors, screwdriver, corkscrew, file, and a final mystery implement that no one can fathom how to use.

2. **Matches** are fine if you remember to keep them in a waterproof container, but a good, windproof lighter is preferable. And a Zippo won't let you down; fill it up with lighter fluid and take a spare flint.

3. **A flashlight** is absolutely essential. And if two or more of you are camping, a flashlight each is a good idea—one can be used to illuminate the tent while the other lights the way for the inevitable late-night call of nature. If the batteries are old, remember to take spares.

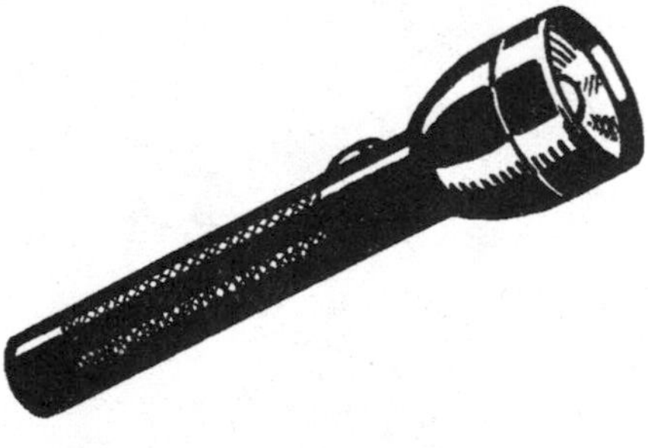

4. A very basic **first aid kit** complete with a roll of band-aids, a pair of nail scissors, and a small tube of antiseptic cream for cuts, bites, and stings will see you right.

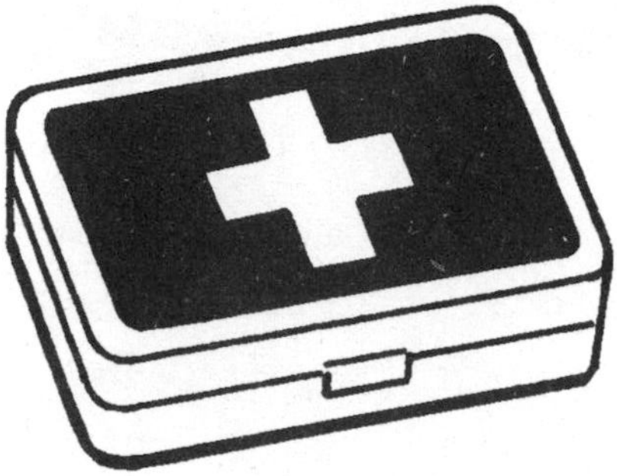

5. **A detailed map of the area** is helpful if you want to go wandering. For exploring further afield, take a compass too.

6. **A toothbrush and toothpaste** might sound obvious but you'll kick yourself if you forget yours—nobody's mouth likes to rough it.

7. Finally, I always find it a comfort to carry a length of **string**. You never know when you might need it.

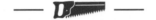

Pitching a Tent

Fortunately, pitching a tent is an easier undertaking than it used to be, for the days of "sleeping under canvas" long ago gave way to "sleeping under polyurethane-coated nylon." That may lack a certain poetry, but it beats hiking home under the weight of a dripping-wet canvas—after a mile of that you might as well have brought the house. The modern, lightweight models are easier to pitch too, and there are even pop-up tents that virtually erect themselves. Whatever the tent, the following old-fashioned advice on pitching will still stand you in good stead.

1. Before your trip, practise assembling and dismantling the tent in the garden to familiarize yourself with the process. This will save time when you arrive at the camp tired and hungry. It'll also ensure that all the poles and pegs you need are packed. If you don't have a garden, practise in your local park. The walk there will give you a feel for the weight too—useful if you plan to hike with the tent.

2. Plan your trip so that you arrive well before darkness falls. Aside from the difficulty of pitching by flashlight, you may awaken to find you've chosen an unsuitable site. Golfers are territorial creatures and have no sense of humor.

3. Choose as flat a patch of ground as possible and clear it of any stones or twigs that could damage the tent and ruin your well-earned slumber. Steer clear of

pitching at the bottom of a hill or valley, or any spot that rainwater is likely to drain into. Face the tent door away from the wind and downhill, if you're on a slight slope. That way rainwater will drain away from the tent opening. Look for a pitch that will be in shade when the sun is at its highest as tents can get very hot in the sun; you don't want your precious provisions to start cooking while you're out walking.

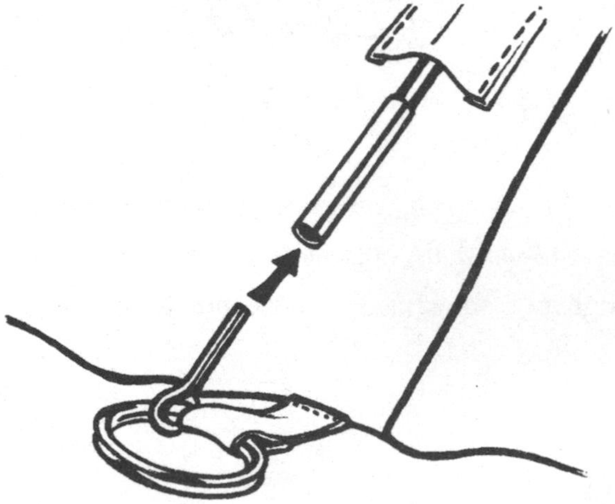

4. When erecting the tent, peg out the corners first and peg the guy ropes taut to maximize the space inside the tent. When feeding poles through the fabric, take your time and be gentle to avoid tearing.

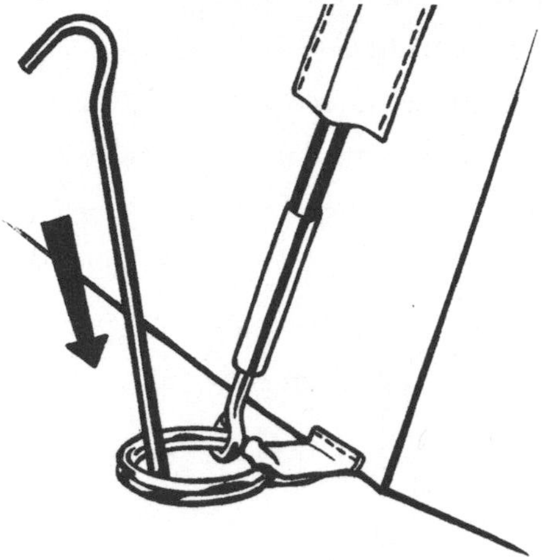

When knocking in tent pegs, remember you're going to have to get them out again, and make sure to leave enough peg showing for the ropes to stand clear of the ground.

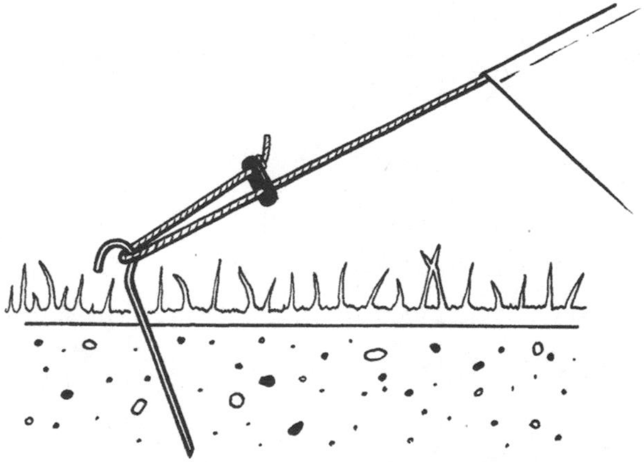

5. Most tents sit on top of a separate waterproof groundsheet. When the tent is up, fold and tuck the edges of the groundsheet under the tent to prevent rainwater from getting between the two.

6. When the time to leave approaches, try to dry the tent off in the sun before packing it. If equipment must be packed damp, dry it as soon as you get home. Don't be tempted to leave it packed as the dampness may damage the materials, which could encourage your tent to develop mildew or even rot.

Building a Campfire

A camp without a fire is as much use as a dinner party without food. Some campsites forbid campfires, but there are others that do permit them in a designated area, so make sure you check before booking.

The key thing to remember when building your campfire is to ensure the wood is bone dry. Slightly damp logs will burn in time, but not before emitting plumes of thick smoke; this smoke will blow straight into your face, regardless of wind direction and however many times you move round the fire. If only damp wood can be found, all is not lost: simply strip the outer bark with a sharp knife until you reach the inside of the log that's dry enough to burn. You should only collect wood that has fallen to the ground, which in some cases may require permission from the landowner, so keep an eye out for signs. Dead wood can play an important ecological role in woodland habitats. Where you are discouraged from collecting it, you will usually find logs are on sale.

Tools and materials

a large container of water
a collection of each of the following:
tinder (any bone-dry material that will catch alight easily, such as dried grass or straw, dead leaves, and pine cones)
kindling (thin, dry sticks that snap easily)
fuel (small, dry logs a few inches thick. Avoid anything large—you'll be waiting all night for them to burn)
a lighter
a long stick

1. Obviously, safety must be your first consideration when lighting a campfire. Be sure to position it 10 to 15 feet away from any tents, fences, dry grass, trees, tree roots, or anything that may be flammable. Never leave the fire unattended, keep a large container of water nearby, and do not, under any circumstances, be tempted to pour gasoline or similarly flammable liquids on to it. Where there is a designated pit, use it. If there is no designated area but there is evidence of a previous fire, clear away the remains and reuse the same site.

Tinder

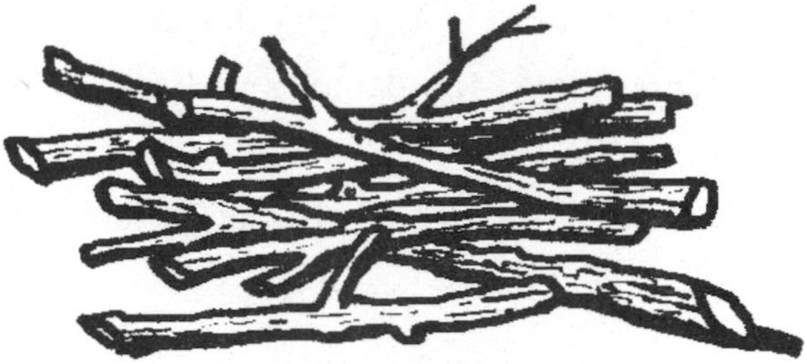

Kindling

Fuel

2. There are various designs or "lays" of campfire, but the simple but effective "tepee" lay is a good one for beginners. First you will need to collect three types of material: tinder, kindling, and fuel. Tinder starts the fire, which sets alight to the kindling. The kindling in turn lights the fuel.

3. Place the tinder in the middle of the fire pit and position the kindling in a tepee shape around it. Then build a larger tepee around the first with the thinnest logs of fuel wood. Be sure to leave plenty of gaps to allow air to circulate and feed the flames and leave a space to access the tinder. Light the tinder from below. When the fire gets going you can add the larger fuel logs.

4. When at last you hear the call of the sleeping bag and the flames are low, you should extinguish the fire. Resist the temptation to pour all your water on at once—it's unlikely to put the fire out, but will produce a lot of smoke! Pouring on a little at a time is the key. Use a long stick to stir the water into the ashes. It can take quite a while to put the fire out completely but it is important to do so. When it no longer emits any heat you can leave it safely. In the morning, clean out all the ash and scatter it discreetly, leaving the pit ready to be used again.

THE CAR

In the first decades of the twentieth century, cars were extravagant playthings for the very wealthy, but mass production meant they were a familiar sight by the 1930s. Doubtless sexist jokes about female drivers were firmly established by this point too, but what was perhaps less well publicized was the significant role women, or one woman in particular, had already played in automotive history. While Karl Benz is generally regarded as the inventor of the automobile, it was his wife, Bertha, who made the first road trip in one of the machines in 1888. And she must have been quite taken with it as she is reputed to have made the journey without her husband's permission. Shocking!

Thankfully, cars (and attitudes) have changed a great deal since then, but affection towards them has always been mixed. To some, cars are merely a necessary evil; to others they're almost part of the family. But however you view your car, it's important to maintain it regularly. And the more you can do yourself, the less you'll have to endure the extortionate prices generally charged by garage mechanics. Major work is best left to the professionals but there's much you can do in the way of routine maintenance. Every model is different and the following instructions are general, so make sure you refer to the manual specific to your vehicle before attempting any of the tasks covered here.

Checking the Oil

To run smoothly, your car needs the right amount of oil—too little can cause extra wear and permanent damage; too much may result in leakage. It's quick and simple to check your oil and you should aim to do it weekly.

Draining and replacing the oil and fitting a new oil filter is a simple but fairly fiddly and dirty task, which I'd recommend leaving to the professionals (it should be included when you have your car serviced).

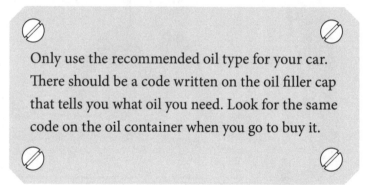

Only use the recommended oil type for your car. There should be a code written on the oil filler cap that tells you what oil you need. Look for the same code on the oil container when you go to buy it.

Tools and equipment

motor oil

a clean rag

1. To read the oil level accurately the car should be on level ground, and make sure you carry out the check after the engine has been turned off for a while. Use your manual to locate the dipstick and the oil filler cap.

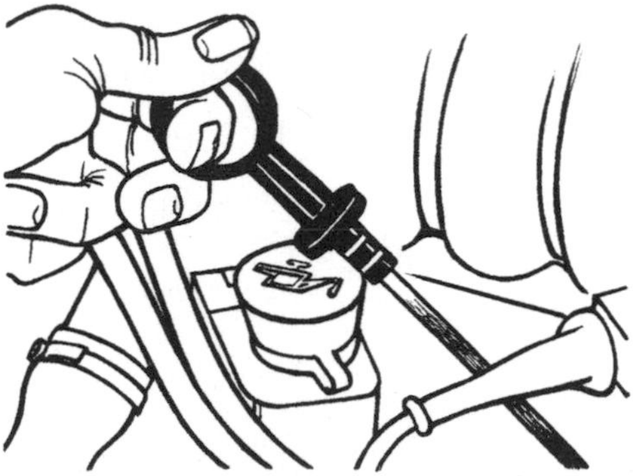

2. Pull out the dipstick and wipe off the oil with a rag. Reinsert the dipstick and pull it out again to check the level. The oil should come up to between the L and the F (low and full) marks. If it's near low, you should top it up.

3. To top it up, unscrew the oil filler cap and carefully pour in a small amount of oil. Give it a few minutes to drain into the oil pan then recheck the level with the dipstick. Repeat until the level is good, adding a little at a time to avoid overfilling.

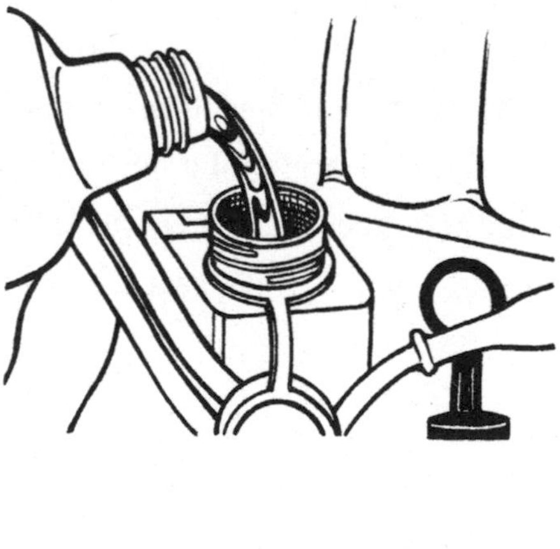

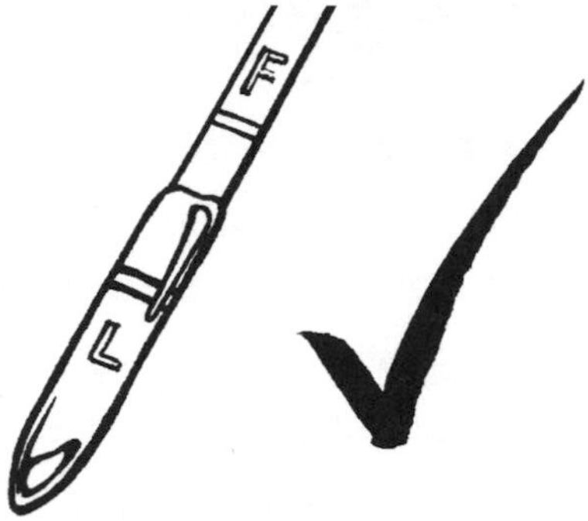

4. While you're checking the oil, take note of its colour and clarity. It should be clear and golden. If it has turned black it's time for an oil change.

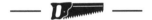

Changing the Air Filter

Your car needs air in order to start. It mixes with the fuel you put into your car to make a combustible vapor, which is then ignited by a spark from the spark plug. When the vapor explodes it forces a piston down a cylinder, and this transfer of chemical energy to mechanical movement is repeated hundreds of times per minute to make the engine run. The air filter is there to prevent dirt and dust mixing with the air, so, like any filter, it will become dirty and clogged over time, which will mean less air will get through.

Check your manual before attempting the change the filter because it will give specific instructions on how to locate and replace it, and how often this should be done.

Tools and equipment

a new air filter (check car manual for correct model)
a clean rag

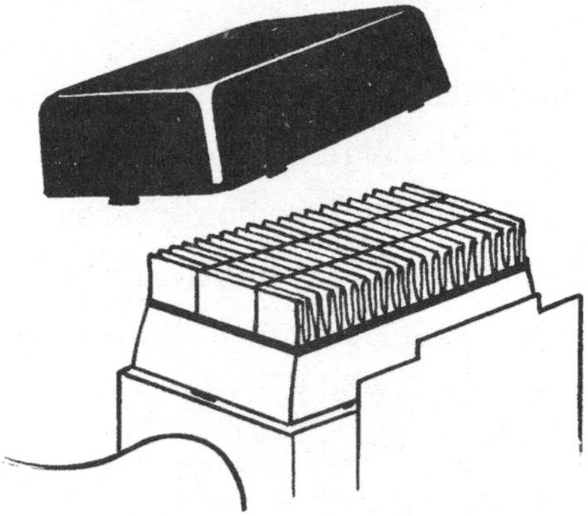

1. Check your manual, as it will give specific instructions on how to locate and replace the air filter.
2. It's usually a quick and straightforward matter of unscrewing or unclipping the old filter and replacing it in the same manner. It's important to ensure that the new filter is fitted well to keep out unwanted grit and grime.

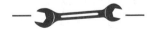

Checking the Coolant

Coolant or antifreeze is usually located to one side of the engine in a translucent plastic reservoir containing a blue, pink, or green liquid. A combination of antifreeze and water, this mixture keeps the engine from overheating and also prevents it from freezing in cold weather. Run this check weekly.

Tools and equipment

coolant or antifreeze (check car manual for correct type)
a funnel
a clean rag

Safety First

Remember to take great care when handling antifreeze—it's poisonous to both humans and animals and even a small spillage can cause trouble.

1. Make sure you carry out any checks when the engine is completely cool.
2. Locate the coolant and check the levels. It should sit between the lines marked max/min or full/low, so if it doesn't it might be time to top it up. Once again, consult your owner's manual to find out which type of coolant is recommended.

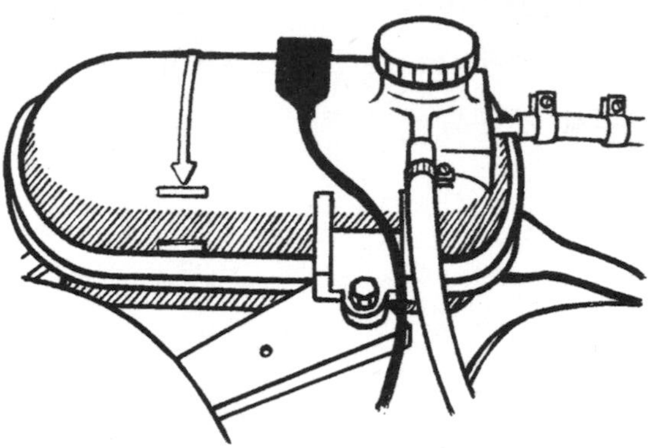

Checking the Brake Fluid

It goes without saying that if you think there's a problem with your brakes you should seek professional advice immediately. But you can help keep any problems at bay by checking the brake fluid levels as part of your routine weekly maintenance.

Tools and equipment

brake fluid (check brake fluid reservoir cap for correct type)
a damp cloth
gloves

Too Hot to Handle

Brake fluid is highly corrosive so make sure you wear a pair of gloves when handling it.

1. Begin by consulting the manual for the specifics of your car. This is particularly important if your car has anti-lock braking (ABS), as the manual may list additional checks.

2. Generally, the brake fluid reservoir is located to the rear of the engine bay on the driver's side. Writing on the top of the cap should tell you which type of fluid to use, usually DOT3 or DOT4 (DOT stands for Department of Transportation; the number refers to the viscosity of the fluid).

3. You may be able to see the fluid level through the plastic but this can be misleading, as brake fluid stains, so it's better to take a look inside. Before removing the cap, clean it and the reservoir well with a damp cloth to minimize the chance of any dirt getting into the system.

4. If needed, fill the reservoir up with brake fluid nearly to the top and replace the cap firmly and straight away. Replace the cap on the bottle of fluid immediately too as brake fluid absorbs moisture easily and should not be left exposed to the air.

Changing a Flat Tire

In case of a tire blowout or puncture, it's essential to carry a spare tire in your car. In most models you will find it in a compartment beneath the trunk, along with the jack and the lug wrench. As soon as you are aware of a flat tire it's wise to attend to it immediately; you shouldn't drive any further on the rim of the wheel as this is both hazardous and potentially damaging to the car.

Tools and equipment

reflective warning triangles
a spare tire
a jack
a lug wrench
a chock

1. Drive to the nearest safe spot, ideally off the road, such as a shoulder or gas station. If no such refuge is available and you must stop on the highway, switch on your hazard warning lights, and place a reflective warning triangle at a sensible distance to the rear of the car. The car should be on firm and level ground with the handbrake on and in reverse gear, or "park" if you drive an automatic. It should also be empty of passengers and pets.

Spare tire

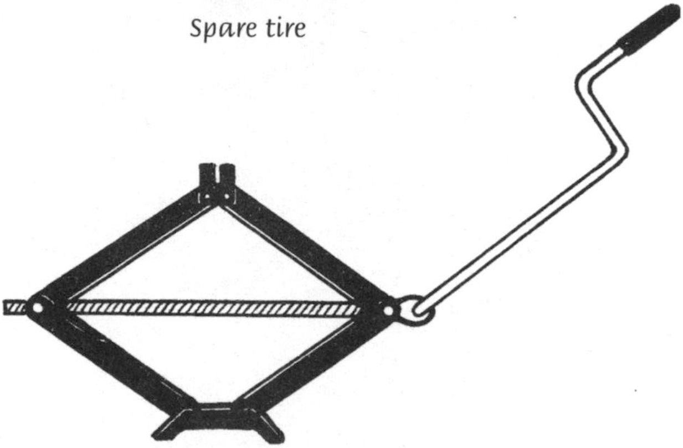

Jack

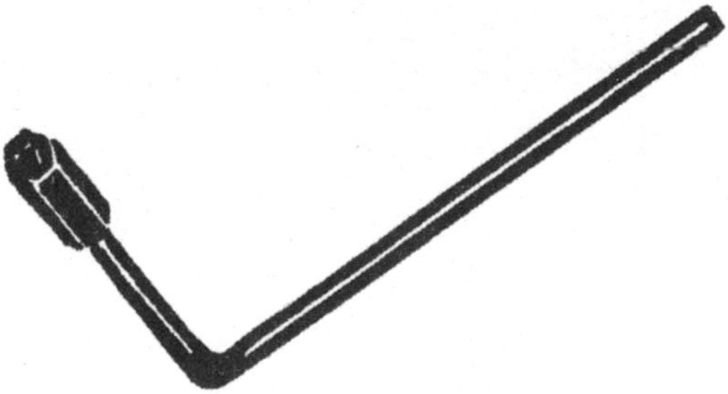

Lug wrench

2. Remove the spare wheel, the jack, and the brace from the trunk. Put a chock (a brick or a rock will also do) behind the back tire if you are changing a front tire (and vice versa if changing the front) to prevent rolling. Place the jack beneath the car, close to the flat tire.

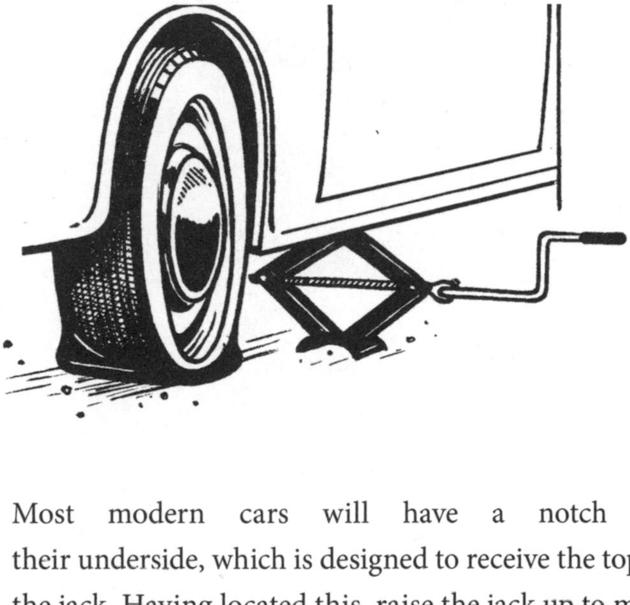

3. Most modern cars will have a notch on their underside, which is designed to receive the top of the jack. Having located this, raise the jack up to meet the notch, but do not yet raise the car.

4. Remove the hubcap (if applicable), then, using the brace, loosen the wheel nuts by turning them counterclockwise. This will require some force, so position yourself over the lug wrench to use your full weight. Loosen the nuts until you can turn them by hand, but don't remove them entirely.

5. Lift the car by slowly turning the jack handle clockwise until the flat tire is clear of the ground, remembering to keep your feet, knees, and anything else clear of the underside of the car, lest the jack slip or fail. Remove the wheel and place it to the rear of the car. Now lift the spare into place and replace the nuts. Tighten them first by hand then further with the lug wrench, but exert no force while the car is still on its jack. You may now lower the car and remove the jack.

6. Fully tighten the nuts in a star formation, starting with one, followed by its opposite, to ensure they're evenly secured. Congratulations—you've successfully changed a tire. Now you can pack away the equipment and continue on your journey (and don't forget that triangle!).

7. At the earliest opportunity you should visit a garage or tire fitters to have the tire mended, replaced, or re-fitted, with a spare stowed safely in its place. Be sure the spare is in good condition, is correctly inflated, and that you have the appropriate type of tire for your car and the conditions you expect it to endure. Tire types should never be mixed as this can be extremely dangerous, so it's wise to seek professional advice on this matter.

BICYCLE MAINTENANCE

There are now thought to be twice as many bicycles as cars in the world, which is probably due in a large part to their ubiquity in China, home to approximately 500 million of the Flying Pigeon brand alone. With that many bikes around, locating your own after work must be a job in itself.

Styles of bike vary according to the activity: there are ever lighter, more aerodynamic models for racing; more durable ones for throwing yourself down the side of a mountain at breakneck speed; commuters opt for the curious-looking folding bicycles, and you might have spotted the BMXs favoured by the young. Despite these vagaries, this chapter is for those who use their bikes for more sedate, everyday activities. See page 160 for a diagram so you can familiarize yourself with the parts of your machine.

The Repair Kit

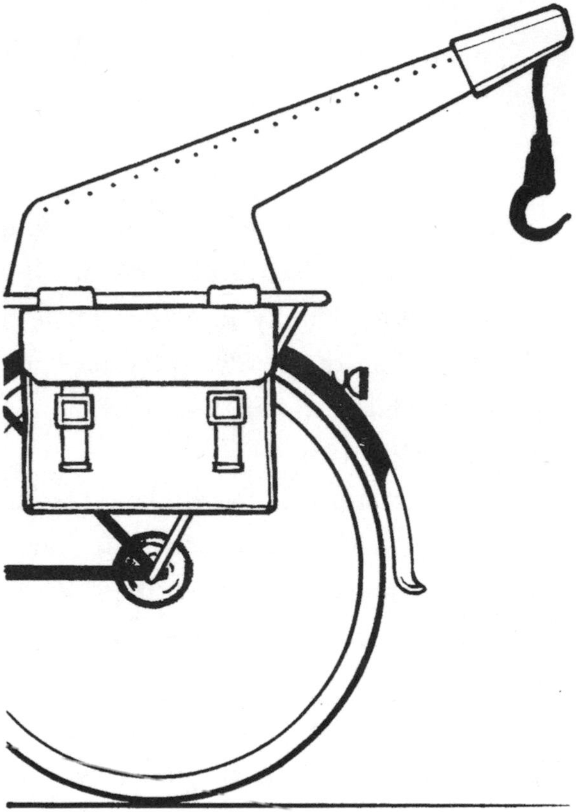

A basic repair kit will fit quite easily into either a backpack or a compact pannier fixed to the bike. Here's a list of the essentials:

1. **A pump:** if you don't have a pump attached to the frame of your bike, carry a mini version in your kit.
2. **A puncture repair kit:** comes in a pocket-sized container and contains the patches, chalk, and adhesive needed to repair a puncture at the roadside.
3. **A spare inner tube:** if you don't relish the idea of mending a puncture in the rain, carry one of these as it will mean you need only swap the tubes, inflate the tire, and cycle home, where you can mend the other tube indoors.
4. **Tire iron**: a set of three will enable you to lever the tire off the wheel with ease.

5. **Wrenches:** a single 8-way wrench should fit all the bolts you may need to deal with.

6. **A screwdriver:** a ratchet screwdriver (see page 20) is ideally compact.
7. **Allen keys**: many newer bikes have bolts that can be adjusted using an Allen key (sometimes referred to as a hex key). Most bike shops sell small multi-tools that contain every size of Allen key you'll need, not to mention tire irons, screwdrivers, and so on.

8. **Lubricant:** small bottle designed specifically for bicycles. This keeps moving parts running smoothly and can also help to loosen bolts that have become stiff.

9. **An old rag:** a weightless bit of kit you will be very glad of.

Routine Maintenance

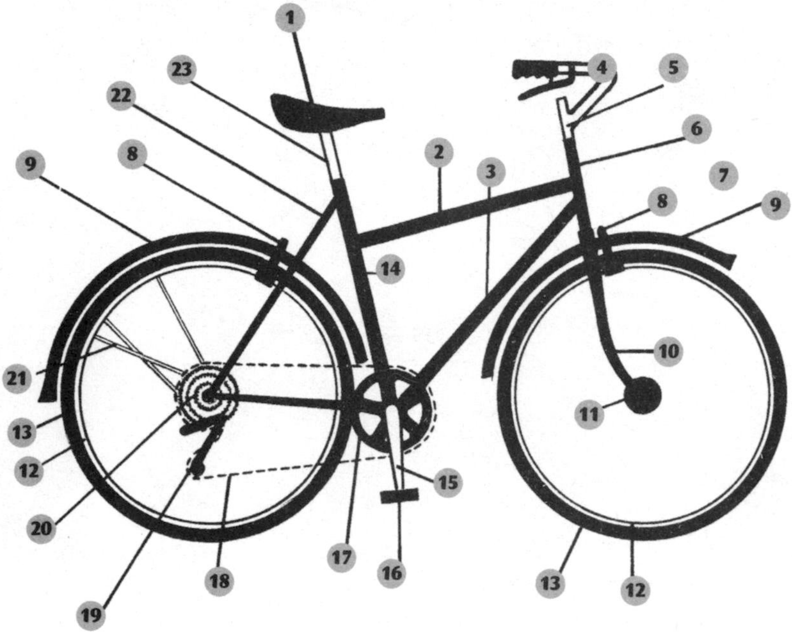

1. Saddle
2. Top tube
3. Down tube
4. Brake lever
5. Handlebar
6. Stem
7. Head tube
8. Brake
9. Mudguard or fender
10. Fork
11. Hub
12. Rim
13. Tire
14. Seat tube
15. Crank
16. Pedal
17. Chainring or chainwheel
18. Chain
19. Derailleur
20. Sprockets or freewheel cassette
21. Spoke
22. Seat stay
23. Seat post

Each time you cycle it's good to get into the habit of giving your tires and brakes a quick check before you set off. If you use your bike regularly, a monthly check-up is advisable.

Tools and equipment

a basin of warm, soapy water
a sponge
a basin of clean water
an old clean rag
a stiff brush (such as a nail brush)
a new toothbrush
bike lubricant

1. Give the old beast a good clean. As with any machine, the cleaner it is, the more smoothly it will run and the longer it will last. A thorough clean also affords you the chance to check for any wear and tear. A simple wash with warm soapy water (dish soap liquid is fine) followed by a rinse or hose down with clean water and a thorough dry with an old rag should have your bike looking good as new. A few points to bear in mind:

   a. Avoid abrasive scourers for the paintwork and chrome; a sponge or a soft brush will do the job.
   b. For the mechanical bits (the sprockets, derailleur, etc.) use a separate, stiffer brush.

c. Floss between the sprockets with a rag.
d. Pay particular attention to cleaning the chain because dirt and grit trapped between the links will speed up wear to the sprockets. A new toothbrush (an old one is too ineffective) will come in handy for cleaning the chain. If it or any other moving parts are particularly gunked up use a chain degreaser, available from cycle stores. Rinse off well after cleaning.

2. Once your bike is squeaky clean and completely dry, it's time to lubricate the moving parts. Work your way around the chain, making sure a drop of lubricant gets between every link. When lubricating the other moving parts, such as gears, try not to overdo it otherwise you will soon have a build-up of gunk. Take care to avoid getting any lubricant on the wheel rims or brake blocks.

3. Now it's time to check the bike all over:

   a. Check the tires for wear and damage and make sure the brake blocks aren't too worn and only touch the wheel rims (not the tires) when you brake.
   b. Ensure the saddle is still aligned with the frame.
   c. Give any screws and bolts a little tighten where needed.
   d. Take a short spin around the block to check the gears are shifting comfortably.

Checking for Chain Wear or "Stretch"

The links on a bike chain are connected by small pins (or rivets). As the chain is drawn around the sprocket (the teethed wheel) it flexes and wears the pins, which in time will slacken the chain, giving the impression that it has stretched. And if the chain doesn't fit snugly on the sprocket, the sprocket's teeth will eventually wear. It's important, therefore, to check the chain and sprocket every few months.

Tools and equipment

a 12-inch ruler

1. There's a simple way to check if the chain has worn out. You'll need a 12-inch ruler and good eyesight. One complete link of the chain should measure an inch as shown here:

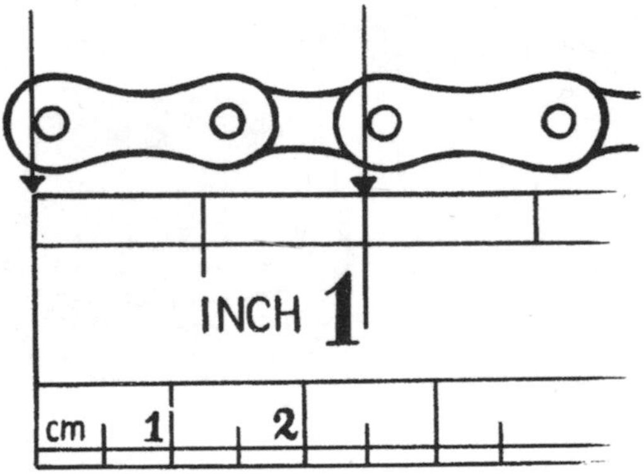

2. Any wear will be too fine to detect by measuring just one link, but you can see the damage if you measure across twelve. The 12-inch mark should center with the last pin. Up to $^{1}/_{16}$ inch out is OK, but more tells you that the chain should be replaced. See page 175 or instructions on replacing the chain.

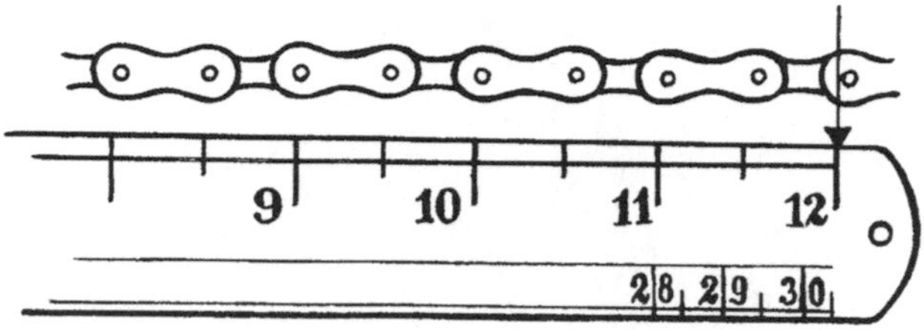

Mending a Puncture

Whether you cycle on or off road, it's almost inevitable that a thorn, a piece of glass, or a sharp little stone will do its worst. The puncture repair kit you've been carrying all this time has been waiting to make its debut and now is the time.

Tools and equipment

a puncture repair kit
tire irons
a wrench
a pump

1. Wheel the bike to a safe spot and lay out your repair kit, tire irons, wrench, and pump.
2. Inspect the injured tire and hunt down the culprit. Once you find it, ease it out gently, and continue to check the rest of the tire—there may have been more than one point of entry, especially if glass or thorns are to blame.

3. Remove the wheel. Some newer types have quick-release bolts; others require a wrench. Just remember, if you do remove any bolts, put them straight into your pocket to avoid losing them. Ease off the wheel and locate the valve on the rim. Unscrew the little plastic cap and put it in your pocket (along with any bolts). If the tire hasn't fully deflated, let out any remaining air by gently pushing a matchstick or the tip of a key into the valve.

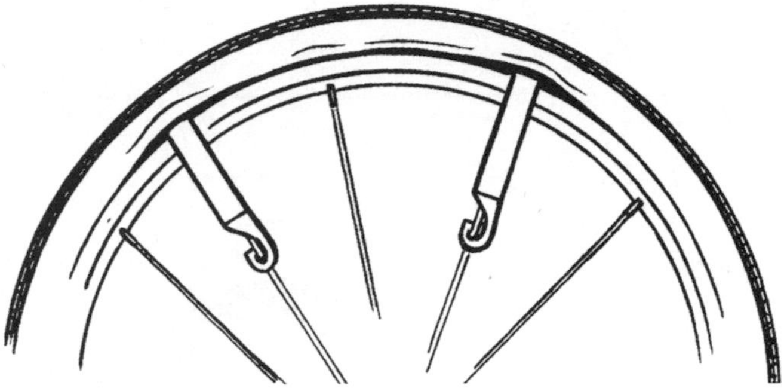

4. Very gently, lever the wall of the tire over the rim and hook the other end of the tire iron on to a spoke. Do the same with a second iron and then a third, about 6-inches apart. Remove the middle iron and continue working round until the whole side of the tire hangs over the rim. Push the valve inside the rim and gently ease out the inner tube. Carefully check all around the inside of the tire to ensure that nothing sharp remains.

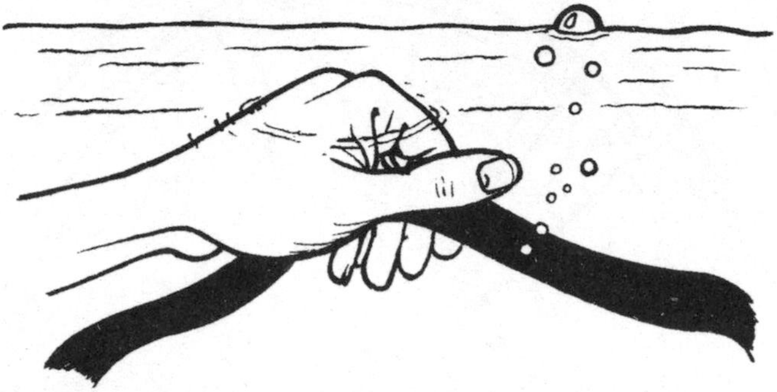

5. Check the inner tube for signs of damage. If you can't locate the hole by eye, pump the tube up and locate it either by the sound or feel of the air escaping. Or, if you have access to water, you can submerge the tube and keep an eye out for escaping bubbles. Once you've found the hole, mark the offending spot with the chalk or a spot of the rubber solution from your repair kit.

6. Deflate the tube and use the file or sandpaper to roughen the area around the hole. Take out the patch from your kit. Apply a fine layer of rubber solution slightly larger than the patch. Let the solution dry for a few minutes then apply the patch as you would a band-aid. Press it down evenly to the edges and hold it in place until you're happy that you have a good seal. If the solution is still a little tacky, crumble a bit of chalk dust over it—this will prevent it from sticking to the inside of the tire.

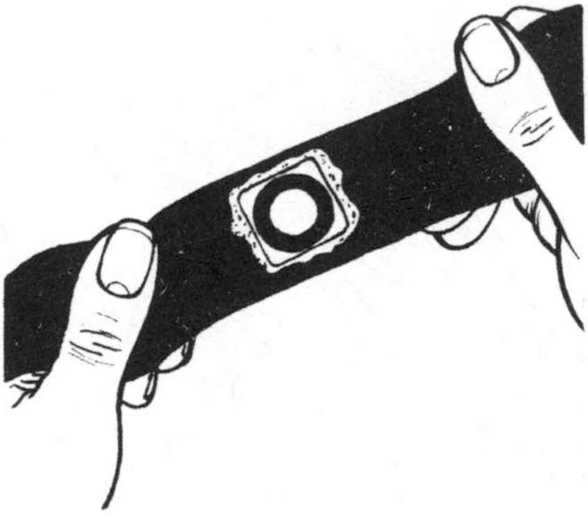

7. Now to replace the tube. Ease the tube into the wheel rim. Be sure to line up the air valve with the hole in the rim and push the valve through the hole. Ease the rest of the tube into the rim and inflate it slightly. This should help to prevent the tube being pinched as you refit the tire. Ease the tire wall back into the rim all round using your thumbs and a tire iron, if necessary, and take great care not to nip the inner tube at any point. Use the markings on the tire walls to be sure that the tire sits on the rim evenly all the way round.

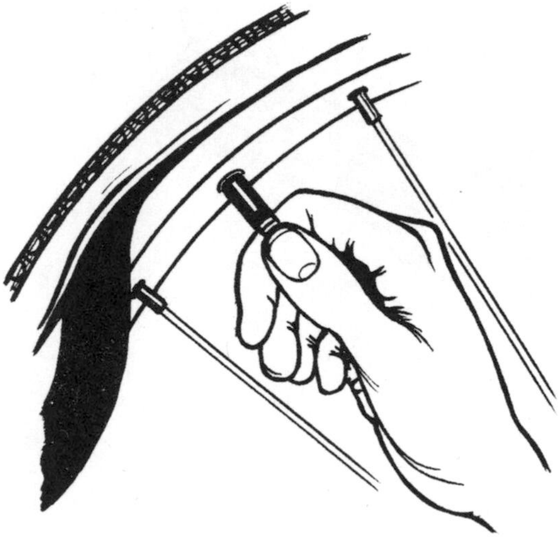

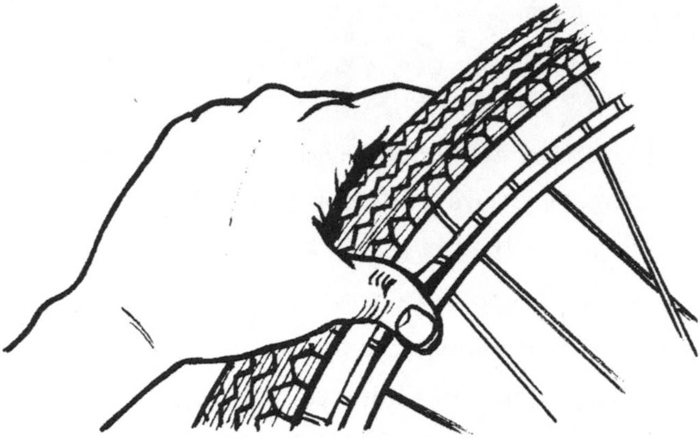

8. Fully reinflate the tire and replace the valve cap. Replace the wheel, ensuring that the rim and brake blocks align as they should. Now you're ready to pack up and get back in the saddle.

Under Pressure

One of the most overlooked issues with tires is their correct pressure. The recommended pressure is written on the tire wall in PSI (pounds per square inch). You can buy a hand-held pressure gauge at most cycling shops and they are incorporated into some pumps. By keeping your tires at the correct pressure, punctures are less likely and you'll have a safer, more comfortable ride.

Replacing the Chain

This task is trickier to describe than it actually is to perform. Although it requires a specific chain-splitting tool, it's a straightforward process to perform. The only other piece of equipment used is a short off-cut of stiff wire, which, although not essential, will make life easier. Any job involving the chain is oily work, so keep an old rag to hand and don't do this on the new white carpet.

It's a really good idea to keep up regular checks on your chain and carry out this fiddly but simple task as soon as it's needed. Ignoring it will result in worn-out sprockets—a much bigger job to replace.

Tools and equipment

stiff wire
a chain-splitting tool
an old rag

1. Use the wire to ease the tension on a section of chain as shown. Now use the splitter to push one of the pins SLOWLY through the chain. You do not want the pin to go all the way through as it will be nigh-on impossible to get it back in. The pin is the width of the chain so you should be able to tell when it's nearly through.

You may have to wiggle the link a little to free it. Before you remove the chain, study the route it takes through the derailleur (sketch it if need be) so you know where to feed the new chain. Keeping hold of the chain, remove the wire and take off the chain.

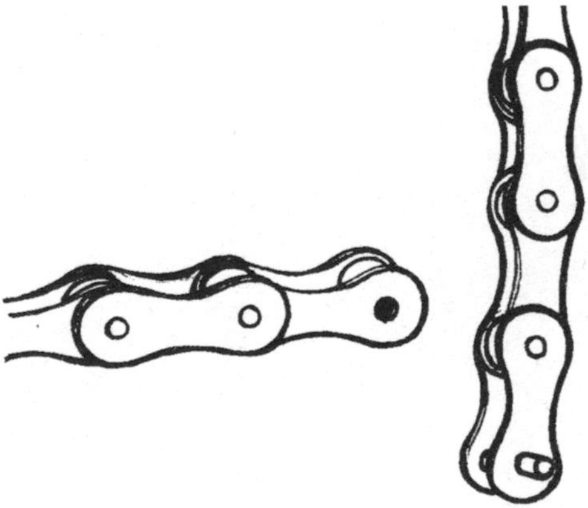

2. Take the new chain and feed it through the derailleur (as per your sketch) and around the front sprocket. Use the wire to connect the chain, leaving a few links hanging. Open the chain-splitter fully. Line up the ends of the chain and very gently start to wind in the pin. If the pin goes too far in, simply turn the splitter round and tweak the pin the other way. If the join feels a little stiff, gentle manipulation from side to side should get it flexing normally.

Brake Maintenance

Efficient brakes are as important on a bicycle as revolving wheels. Long ago on the Scottish island of Arran, my mother and I explored the beautifully rugged and mountainous scenery on a pair of bikes. I was only a boy of about ten, but the outing has stayed with me, not least because on the steepest of our descents my mum decided to test her brakes. High winds prevented me from hearing precisely what she was yelling as she hurtled past, but I imagine it pertained to mechanical failure. Being a resourceful woman, she substituted a steep bank for the braking system and the bicycle came to a safe halt. A little later, by some miracle, so did she.

It is my duty, therefore, to pass on the following information so you may not make the same mistakes as my freewheeling mother. Although brakes are covered in the section on routine maintenance (see page 160), a little more information here may be useful. The following instructions apply to standard caliper brakes.

Adjusting the blocks

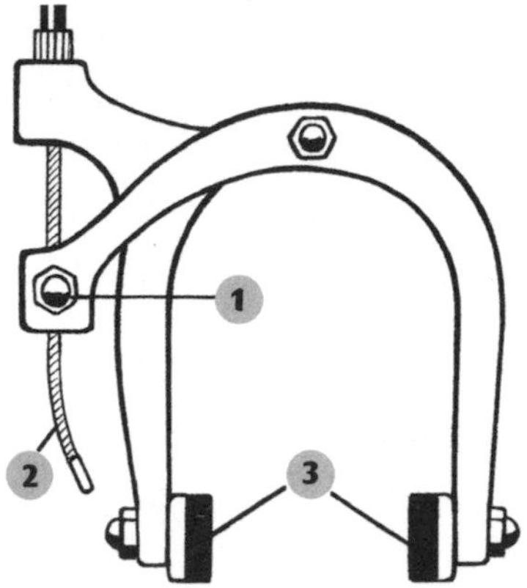

1. Cable-fixing bolt
2. Brake cable
3. Brake blocks

To ensure your brakes perform as they should you must ensure they're positioned correctly—in the center of the rim and not touching the tire, or overhanging the rim.

1. The brake blocks are held in place by a small nut. Loosen it with a wrench so that the brake block can be moved up and down.
2. The brakes need to be engaged to determine when the block is in the right position. It helps to have a second pair of hands working the brake lever.

Replacing the blocks

Most blocks are marked with a line to indicate when they are worn to the point of replacement.

1. To remove the old blocks you must release the tension on the brake cable by unscrewing the cable-fixing bolt. You may now completely remove the brake block and change it.
2. Reconnect the brake cable and adjust.

Cable adjustment

By tightening the brake cable the brakes will engage more quickly as you pull the brake lever.

1. Unscrew the cable-fixing bolt a little to allow movement when you tug the cable. Pull the cable tight and retighten the bolt.
2. If your problem is that the brakes engage too quickly, do the same but slacken the cable instead of tightening it.

Bibliography

Master Basic DIY by DIY Doctor (Teach Yourself, 2010)

Reader's Digest DIY Manual (Reader's Digest, 2011)

Hayne's Home Plumbing Manual: The Complete Step-by-Step Guide by Andy Blackwell (J.H. Haynes & Co. Ltd., 2012)

RHS Plants for Places (Dorling Kindersley, 2011)

Be Prepared: How to Light a Wet Match and 199 Other Useful Things to Know by the Scout Association (Simon & Schuster, 2013)

How to Grill by Steven Raichlen (Workman Publishing, 2002)

Car Care Made Easy: The Ultimate Glovebox Companion by Alex Moss (Active Paper Ltd., 2010)

Bike Repair Manual by Chris Sidwells (Dorling Kindersley, 2011)

Index